Debbie Bliss
Great Knits for Kids

27 Classic Designs for Infants to Ten-Year-Olds

Trafalgar Square Publishing

North Pomfret, Vermont

For my mother, Mid

This revised edition published in 2005
Reprinted in 2006

First published in the United States of America in 1997
by Trafalgar Square Publishing, North Pomfret, Vermont 05053

Printed and bound in Singapore by Kyodo Printing Co Ltd

9 8 7 6 5 4 3 2

Library of Congress Control Number: 2004106701

ISBN-13: 978-1-57076-301-4
ISBN-10: 1-57076-301-1

Conceived, edited and designed by Collins & Brown Limited
Designed and typeset: Smith & Gilmour, London
Photography: Sandra Lousada
Reproduction by Classicscan Pte Ltd, Singapore

We recommend that you use Rowan yarns for the patterns in this book.
There is, however, information on substituting other yarns on page 8.

Contents

Introduction 7
Basic Information 8

Tunic Top with Bobble Detail 10
Cable and Bobble Tunic 14
Cabled, Zipped Jacket with Collar 18
Ribbed Denim Sweater 22
Cream Denim Sweater 26
Denim Fisherman Shirt 30
Ribbed Sweater with Stripes 34
Stocking-stitch Sweater with Collar 38
Lace-edged Cardigan 42
Floral Cardigan 46
Moss-stitch Tunic with Hat 50
Guernsey with Ribbed Yoke 54
Denim Wrap 58
Moss-stitch Beret 60
Aran Sweater 62
Cable and Garter-stitch Sweater 66
Moss and Cable Jacket with Petal Collar 70
Fair Isle Sweater with Two-color Rib 74
Cabled Tunic with Shawl Collar 78
Shawl-collared Jacket with Fair Isle Bands 82
Navy and Cream Striped Top 86
Garter-stitch Jacket 90
Simple Sweater with Shoulder Seam Detail 94
Squirrel Jacket 98
Tweed Jacket with Cable Beret 102
Black and White Fair Isle Cardigan 106
Simple Striped Sweater 110

Suppliers 112

Introduction

Great Knits for Kids is a collection of classic but stylish hand-knits for children, with the designs covering the age range from babies right up to children aged ten. I loved having the opportunity to create designs for seven to ten-year-olds, as exciting, wearable styles for older children can be hard to find.

There are 27 designs to choose from: fisher knits that use traditional stitches in subtly-faded denim yarn, delicate cotton cardigans, classic country house tweeds and a versatile wrap that can double up as a cot cover or a throw.

There is something to suit all knitting abilities, with basic stocking stitch and garter stitch for beginners, texture with cables and bobbles for Aran lovers, and both simple and more intricate Fair Isles for knitters who like to work with color patterning.

As always, depending on the style, I have given some of the designs generous size allowances, as I think that children are used to wearing casual clothes and should feel comfortable and unrestricted when wearing knitwear. However, as all the patterns quote actual measurements, you can knit up whichever size you prefer.

Basic Information

NOTES

Figures for larger sizes are given in () brackets. Where only one figure appears, this applies to all sizes.

Work figures given in [] brackets the number of times stated afterwards. Alternatively, they give the resultant number of stitches.

Where 0 appears, no stitches or rows are worked for this size.

The yarn amounts given in the instructions are based on average requirements and should therefore be considered approximate. If you want to use a substitute yarn, choose a yarn of the same type and weight as the one recommended. The following descriptions of the various Rowan yarns are meant as a guide to the yarn weight and type (i.e. cotton, mohair, wool, etc.). Remember that the description of the yarn weight is only a rough guide and you should always test a yarn first to see if it will achieve the correct tension (gauge).

Magpie Aran: a fisherman medium-weight yarn (100% pure new wool) approx. 150m/164yd per 100g/3 ½oz hank.

Cotton Glace: a lightweight cotton yarn (100% cotton) approx. 112m/123yd per 50g/1 ¾oz ball.

Designer DK: a double knitting-weight yarn (100% pure new wool) approx. 115m/125yd per 50g/1 ¾oz ball.

Handknit DK Cotton: a medium-weight cotton yarn (100% cotton) approx. 85m/90yd per 50g/1 ¾oz ball.

True 4-ply Botany: a 4-ply yarn (100% pure new wool) approx. 170m/220yd per 50g/1 ¾oz ball.

DK Tweed: a double knitting weight yarn (100% pure new wool) approx. 110m/120yd per 50g/1 ¾oz ball.

The amount of a substitute yarn needed is determined by the number of meters/yards needed rather than by the number of grams/ounces. If you are unsure when choosing a suitable substitute, ask your yarn shop to advise you.

TENSION

Each pattern in this book specifies a tension—the number of stitches and rows per centimeter/inch that should be obtained with the given needles, yarn and stitch pattern. Check your tension carefully before commencing work.

Use the same yarn, needles and stitch pattern as those to be used for the main work and knit a sample at least 12.5cm/5in square. Smooth out the finished sample on a flat surface but do not stretch it. To check the tension, place a ruler horizontally on the sample and mark 10cm/4in across with pins. Count the number of stitches between the pins. To check the row tension, place a ruler horizontally on the sample and mark 10cm/4in with pins. Count the number of rows between pins. If the number of stitches and rows is greater than specified, try again using larger needles; if less, use smaller needles.

The stitch tension is the most important element to get right.

The following terms may be unfamiliar to US readers.

UK terms	US terms
Aran wool	'fisherman' (unbleached wool) yarn
ball band	yarn wrapper
cast off	bind off
DK wool	knitting worsted yarn
double crochet stitch	single crochet stitch
make up (garment)	finish (garment)
moss stitch	seed stitch
rib	ribbing
stocking stitch	stockinette stitch
tension	gauge
waistcoat	vest

In the US balls or hanks of yarn are sold in ounces, not in grams; the weights of the relevant Rowan yarns are given on this page.

In addition, a few specific knitting or crochet terms may be unfamiliar to some readers. The list above right explains the abbreviations used in this book to help the reader understand how to follow the various stitches and stages.

STANDARD ABBREVIATIONS

alt = alternate; **beg** = begin(ning); **cont** = continue; **dec** = decreas(e)ing; **foll** = following; **inc** = increas(e)ing; **k** = knit; **m1** = make one by picking up loop lying between st just worked and next st and work into the back of it; **patt** = pattern; **p** = purl; **psso** = pass slipped stitch over; **rem** = remain(ing); **rep** = repeat; **skpo** = sl one, k1, pass slipped st over; **sl** = slip; **st(s)** = stitch(es); **st st** = stocking stitch; **tbl** = through back of loop(s); **tog** = together; **yb** = yarn back; **yf** = yarn forward; **yon** = yarn over needle; **yrn** = yarn round needle.

IMPORTANT

Check on ball band for washing instructions. After washing, pat garments into shape and dry flat away from direct heat.

Rowan Denim will shrink and fade when it is washed, just like a pair of jeans. Unlike many 'denim look' yarns this uses real indigo dye, which only coats the surface of the yarn, leaving a white core that is gradually exposed through washing and wearing.

When washed for the first time, the yarn will shrink by up to one-fifth on length; the width, however, will remain the same. All the necessary adjustments have been made in the instructions for the patterns specially designed for Denim.

The knitted pieces should be washed separately at a temperature of 60–70°C (140–158°F) before sewing the garment together. The pieces can then be tumble-dried. Dye loss will be greatest during the initial wash; the appearance of the garment will, however, be greatly enhanced with additional washing and wearing. The cream denim yarn will shrink in the same way, but will not fade.

Right: Guernsey with Ribbed Yoke (see page 55) and Denim Fisherman Shirt (see page 31).

Tunic Top with Bobble Detail

MATERIALS
10 (11: 11: 12: 13) 50g balls of Rowan Cotton Glace.
Pair each of 2 ¾mm (No 12/US 2) and 3 ¼mm (No 10/US 3) knitting needles.

TENSION
25 sts and 34 rows to 10cm/4in square over st st on 3 ¼mm (No 10/US 3) needles.

ABBREVIATIONS
mb = [k1, p1] 3 times, then k1 all in next st, pass 2nd, 3rd, 4th, 5th, 6th, and 7th st over 1st st. Also see page 8.

BACK
With 2 ¾mm (No 12/US 2) needles, cast on 107 (112: 122: 132: 142) sts.
K5 rows.
Next row: K3, [mb, k4] to last 4 sts, mb, k3.
K3 rows, inc 0 (3: 1: 1: 3) sts on last row.
107 (115: 123: 133: 145) sts.
Change to 3 ¼mm (No 10/US 3) needles.
1st row: K.
2nd row: K7, p to last 7 sts, k7.
3rd row: K3, mb, k to last 4 sts, mb, k3.
4th row: As 2nd row.
5th and 6th rows: As 1st and 2nd rows.
Rep last 6 rows once more, then work 1st and 2nd rows again.
Cont in st st across all sts until Back measures 32 (34: 38: 40: 43)cm/12 ½ (13 ¼: 15: 15 ½: 16 ¾)in from beg, ending with a k row.
Next row: P5 (5: 6: 6: 6), k5, p to last 10 (10: 11: 11: 11) sts, k5, p to end.
Next row: K.
Rep last 2 rows until Back measures 40 (44: 48: 52: 55)cm/15 ¾ (17 ¼: 19: 20 ½: 21 ¾)in from beg, ending with a wrong side row.
Cont in st st across all sts until Back measures 45 (49: 53: 57: 60)cm17 ¾ (19 ¼: 21: 22 ½: 23 ¾)in from beg, ending with a p row.

Shape Shoulders
Cast off 19 (21: 22: 24: 27) sts at beg of next 2 rows and 20 (21: 23: 25: 27) sts at beg of foll 2 rows. Cast off rem 29 (31: 33: 35: 37)sts.

MEASUREMENTS

To fit age	3–4	4–6	6–8	8–9	9–10	years
Actual chest measurement	86	92	98	106	116	cm
	34	36	38 ½	41 ½	45 ½	in
Length	45	49	53	57	60	cm
	17 ¾	19 ¼	21	22 ½	23 ¾	in
Sleeve seam	28	30	35	38	40	cm
	11	12	13 ¾	15	15 ¾	in

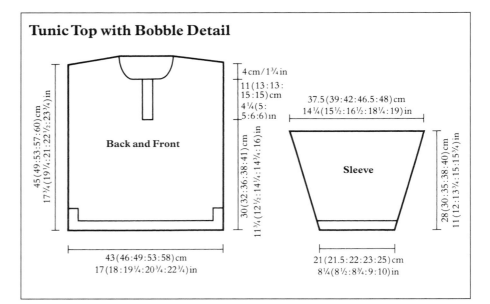

Tunic Top with Bobble Detail

Back and Front

45 (49: 53: 57: 60) cm
17 ¾ (19 ¼: 21: 22 ½: 23 ¾) in

30 (32: 36: 38: 41) cm
11 ¾ (12 ½: 14 ¼: 14 ¾: 16) in

43 (46: 49: 53: 58) cm
17 (18: 19 ¼: 20 ¾: 22 ¾) in

4 cm/1 ¾ in
11 (13: 13: 15: 15) cm
4 ¼ (5: 5: 6: 6) in

Sleeve

37.5 (39: 42: 46.5: 48) cm
14 ¼ (15 ½: 16 ½: 18 ¼: 19) in

28 (30: 35: 38: 40) cm
11 (12: 13 ¾: 15: 15 ¾) in

21 (21.5: 22: 23: 25) cm
8 ¼ (8 ½: 8 ¾: 9: 10) in

FRONT

Work as given for Back until Front measures 30 (32: 36: 38: 41)cm/11 ¾ (12 ½: 14 ¼: 14 ¾: 16)in from beg, ending with a k row.

Divide for opening
Next row: P50 (54: 58: 63: 69), k7, turn.
Work on this set of sts only.
Next row: K.
Next row: P to last 7 sts, k7.
Rep last 2 rows once more.
1st row: K3, mb, k to end.
2nd row: P5 (5: 6: 6: 6), k5, p to last 7 sts, k7.
3rd row: K.
4th row: As 2nd row.
5th and 6th rows: As 3rd and 4th rows.
Rep last 6 rows until Front measures 40 (44: 48: 52: 55)cm/15 ¾ (17 ¼: 19: 20 ½: 21 ¾)in from beg, ending with a wrong side row.
Keeping patt at opening edge correct and working remainder in st st, cont for a further 1cm/¼in, ending at inside edge.

Shape Neck

Cast off 7 st at beg of next row and 4 (4: 4: 5: 5) sts at beg of foll alt row. Dec one st at neck edge on every row until 39 (42: 45: 49: 54) sts remain. Cont straight until Front matches Back to shoulder shaping, ending at side edge.

Shape Shoulder

Cast off 19 (21: 22: 24: 27) sts at beg of next row. Work one row. Cast off rem 20 (21: 23: 25: 27) sts.
With wrong side facing, rejoin yarn to rem sts, k7, p to end.
Next row: K.
Next row: K7, p to end.
Rep last two rows once more.
1st row: K to last 4 sts, mb, k3.
2nd row: K7, p to last 10 (10: 11: 11: 11) sts, k5, p to end.
3rd row: K.
4th row: As 2nd row.
5th and 6th rows: As 3rd and 4th rows.
Complete to match first side.

SLEEVES

With 2 ¾mm (No 12/US 2) needles cast on 47 (47: 52: 52: 57) sts.
K 5 rows.
Next row: K3, [mb, k4] to last 4 sts, mb, k3.
K 5 rows, inc 5 (7: 4: 6: 5) sts evenly across last row. 52 (54: 56: 58: 62) sts.
Change to 3 ¼mm (No 10/US 3) needles.
Beg with a k row, work in st st, inc one st at each end or 3rd row and every foll 3rd (3rd; 4th: 4th: 4th) row until there are 94 (98: 106: 114: 120) sts. Cont straight until Sleeve measures 28 (30: 35: 38: 40)cm/11 (12: 13 ¾: 15: 15 ¾)in from beg, ending with a wrong side row. Cast off.

COLLAR

With 2 ¾mm (No 12/US 2) needles cast on 75 (81: 87: 93: 99) sts. K 3 rows.
Next row: K1, k2 tog, k to last 3 stitches, k2 tog tbl, k1.
K 4 rows. Rep last 5 rows 4 times more. K 5 rows. Cast off.

TO MAKE UP

Join shoulder seams. Catch down the 7 cast on sts on wrong side to base of opening. Sew on sleeves, placing center of sleeves to shoulder seams. Beg at top of borders, join side seams, then sleeve seams. Sew on collar.

Right: Tunic Top with Bobble Detail and Cable and Bobble Tunic (see page 15).

Cable and Bobble Tunic

MATERIALS

12 (13: 14) 50g balls of Rowan Cotton Glace.
Pair each of 3 ¼mm (No 10/US 3) and 3 ¾mm (No 9/US 4) knitting needles.
Cable needle.
3 buttons.

TENSION

29 sts and 36 rows to 10cm/4in square over pattern on 3 ¾mm (No 9/US 4) needles.

ABBREVIATIONS

C4B = sl next 2 sts onto cable needle and leave at back of work, k2, then k2 from cable needle;
Cr3L = sl next 2 sts onto cable needle and leave at front of work, p1, then k2 from cable needle;
Cr3R = sl next st onto cable needle and leave at back of work, k2, then p1 from cable needle;
mb = pick up loop lying between st just worked and next st and work into front, back, front, back and front of the loop, then pass 2nd, 3rd, 4th and 5th st over 1st st. Also see page 8.

BACK

With 3 ¼mm (No 10/US 3) needles, cast on 122 (146: 170) sts.
1st rib row (right side): [P2, k2, p1, k4, p1, k2] to last 2 sts, p2.
2nd rib row: K2, [p2, k1, p4, k1, p2, k2] to end.
3rd rib row: [P1, mb, p1, pass bobble st over the p st just worked, k2, p1, C4B, p1, k2] to last 2 sts, p2.
4th rib row: as 2nd row.
Rib a further 14 rows.
Change to 3 ¾mm (No 9/US 4) needles.
1st row: P1, [mb, p1, pass bobble st over the p st just worked, p3, C4B, p4] to last st, p1.
2nd row: K5, [p4, k8] to last 9 sts, p4, k5.
3rd row: P4, [Cr3R, Cr3L, p6] to last 10 sts, Cr3R, Cr3L, p4.

MEASUREMENTS

To fit age	3–4	6–8	9–10	years
Actual chest measurement	84	100	117	cm
	33	39 ½	46	in
Length	44	52	60	cm
	17 ¼	20 ½	23 ¾	in
Sleeve seam	28	35	41	cm
	11	13 ¾	16	in

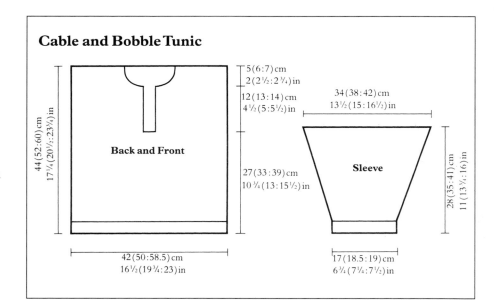

Cable and Bobble Tunic

Back and Front:
44 (52 : 60) cm / 17 ¼ (20 ½ : 23 ¾) in
5 (6 : 7) cm / 2 (2 ½ : 2 ¾) in
12 (13 : 14) cm / 4 ½ (5 : 5 ½) in
27 (33 : 39) cm / 10 ¾ (13 : 15 ½) in
42 (50 : 58.5) cm / 16 ½ (19 ¾ : 23) in

Sleeve:
34 (38 : 42) cm / 13 ½ (15 : 16 ½) in
28 (35 : 41) cm / 11 (13 ¾ : 16) in
17 (18.5 : 19) cm / 6 ¾ (7 ¼ : 7 ½) in

4th row: K4, [p6, k6] to last 10 sts, p6, k4.

5th row: P1, [mb, p1, pass bobble st over the p st just worked, p1, Cr3R, p2, Cr3L, p2] to last st, p1.

6th row: K3, [p8, k4] to last 11 sts, p8, k3.

7th row: P2, [Cr3R, p4, Cr3L, p2] to end.

8th row: K2, [p10, k2] to end.

9th row: P1, [Cr3R, p6, Cr3L] to last st, p1.

10th row: K1, p to last st, k1.

11th row: P1, [Cr3L, p6, Cr3R] to last st, p1.

12th row: As 8th row.

13th row: P2, [Cr3L, p4, Cr3R, p2] to end.

14th row: As 6th row.

15th row: P1, [mb, p1, pass bobble st over the p st just worked, p1, Cr3L, p2, Cr3R, p2] to last st, p1.

16th row: As 4th row.

17th row: P4, [Cr3L, Cr3R, p6] to last 10 sts, Cr3L, Cr3R, p4.

18th row: As 2nd row.

19th and 20th rows: As 1st and 2nd rows.

21st row: P5, [k4, p8] to last 9 sts, k4, p5.

22nd row: As 2nd row.

These 22 rows form patt. Cont in patt until Back measures approximately 27 (33: 39)cm/10 ¾ (13: 15 ½)in from beg, ending with 14th pattern row. Mark each end of last row.**

Omitting making first bobble throughout, cont in patt until Back measures 44 (52: 60)cm/17 ¼ (20 ½: 23 ¾)in from beg, ending with a wrong side row.

Shape Shoulders

Next row: Cast off 42 (52: 62), patt to last 42 (52: 62) sts, cast off these sts.

Leave rem 38 (42: 46) sts on a holder.

FRONT

Work as given for Back to **. Omitting making first bobble throughout, work as follows:

Divide for opening

Next row: Patt 58 (70: 82), cast off next 6 sts, patt to end.

Cont on last set of sts only. Keeping patt correct, work a further 12 (13: 14)cm/4 ½ (5: 5 ½)in, ending at inside edge.

Shape Neck

Cast off 8 (9: 10) sts at beg of next row.

Dec one st at neck edge on next 5 rows then on every foll alt row until 42 (52: 62) sts rem.

Cont straight until Front matches Back to shoulder shaping, ending with a wrong side row. Cast off.

With wrong side facing, rejoin yarn to rem sts and patt to end. Complete as given for first side.

SLEEVES

With 3 ¼mm (No 10/US 3) needles cast on 50 (54: 56) sts.

1st rib row (right side): P0 (0: 1), k0 (2: 2), p2, [k2, p1, k4, p1, k2, p2] to last 0 (2: 3) sts, k0 (2: 2), p0 (0: 1).

2nd rib row: K0 (0: 1), p0 (2: 2), [k2, p2, k1, p4, k1, p2] to last 2 (4: 5) sts, k2, p0 (2: 2), k0 (0: 1).

These two rows set position of rib. Cont in rib to match Back, work a further 16 rows. Change to 3 ¾mm (No 9/US 4) needles.

1st row: P1 (3: 4), [mb, p1, pass bobble st over the p st just worked, p3, C4B, p4] to last 1 (3: 4) sts, mb, p1, pass bobble st over the p st just worked, p0 (2: 3).

2nd row: K5 (7: 8), p4, [k8, p4] to last 5 (7: 8) sts, k5 (7: 8).

These 2 rows set position of patt. Cont in patt, inc one st at each end of next row and every foll 3rd row until there are 98 (110: 122) sts, working inc sts into patt. Cont straight until Sleeve measures 28 (35: 41)cm/11 (13 ¾: 16)in from beg, ending with a wrong side row. Cast off.

NECKBAND

Join shoulder seams.

With 3 ¼mm (No 10/ US 3) needles and right side facing, k up 21 (24: 27) sts up right front neck, k6 (2: 2), k2 tog, [k4 (4: 3), k2 tog] 4 (6: 8) times, k6 (2: 2) across back neck, k up 21 (24; 27) sts down left front neck. 75 (83: 91) sts. K 6 rows. Cast off.

BUTTON BAND

With 3 ¼mm (No 10/US 3) needles and right side of work facing, k up 30 (33: 36) sts along left edge of front opening, including neckband. K 10 rows. Cast off.

BUTTONHOLE BAND

With 3 ¼mm (No 10/ US 3) needles and right side facing, k up 30 (33: 36) sts along right edge of front opening, including neckband, K 3 rows.

***Next row:** K10 (11: 12), turn.

Work on this set of sts only.

Next row: K2 tog, k to last 2 sts, k2 tog tbl.

Next row: K.

Rep last 2 rows until 2 (3: 2) sts rem. Work 2 (3: 2) tog and fasten off. With right side facing, rejoin yarn to rem sts and rep from *** twice more.

TO MAKE UP

Sew on sleeves between markers. Join side and sleeve seams. Catch down row end edge of button band to base of opening. Push large knitting needle through sts on each point of buttonhole band thus forming buttonhole. Sew on button.

Right: Tunic Top with Bobble Detail (see page 11) and Cabled, Zipped Jacket with Collar (see page 19).

Cabled, Zipped Jacket with Collar

MATERIALS

19 (22) 50g balls of Rowan DK Handknit Cotton.
Pair each of 3 ¼mm (No 10/US 3) and 4mm (No 8/US 6) knitting needles.
Cable needle.
45 (55)cm/18 (22)in long open ended zip fastener.

TENSION

27 sts and 29 rows to 10cm/4in square over pattern on 4mm (No 8/US 6) needles.

ABBREVIATIONS

Tw4L = sl next 3 sts onto cable needle and leave at front of work, k1, then k1 tbl, p1, k1 tbl from cable needle;
Tw4R = sl next st onto cable needle and leave at back of work, k1 tbl, p1, k1 tbl, then k1 from cable needle;
mb = [k1, yf, k1, yf, k1] all in next st, turn, p5, turn, k3, k2 tog, then pass 2nd, 3rd and 4th st over 1st st.
Also see page 8.

PANEL A

Worked over 23 sts.
1st row (wrong side) K8, p1, k1, p3, k1, p1, k8.
2nd row P7, Tw4R, k1 tbl, Tw4L, p7.
3rd row K7, p1, [k1, p1] 4 times, k7.
4th row P6, Tw4R, k1, k1 tbl, k1, Tw4L, p6.
5th row K6, p1, k1, p1, [k2, p1] twice, k1, p1, k6.
6th row P5, Tw4R, k2, k1 tbl, k2, Tw4L, p5.
7th row K5, p1, k1, p2, k2, p1, k2, p2, k1, p1, k5.
8th row P4, Tw4R, k1 tbl, [k2, k1 tbl] twice, Tw4L, p4.
9th row K4, p1, [k1, p1] twice, [k2, p1] twice, [k1, p1] twice, k4.
10th row P3, Tw4R, k1, k1 tbl, [k2, k1 tbl] twice, k1, Tw4L, p3.
11th row K3, p1, k1, p1, [k2, p1] 4 times, k1, p1, k3.
12th row P2, Tw4R, k2, [k1 tbl, k2] 3 times, Tw4L, p2.
13th row K2, p1, k1, p1, k3, p1, [k2, p1] twice, k3, p1, k1, p1, k2.
14th row P2, k1 tbl, p1, k1 tbl, k3, mb, [k2, mb] twice, k3, k1 tbl, p1, k1 tbl, p2.
15th row K2, p1, k1, p1, k3, p1 tbl, [k2, p1 tbl] twice, k3, p1, k1, p1, k2.
16th row P2, k1 tbl, p1, k1 tbl, p3, k1 tbl, p1, k3 tbl, p1, k1 tbl, p3, k1 tbl, p1, k1 tbl, p2.
These 16 rows form patt.

MEASUREMENTS

To fit age	4-6	6–8	years
Actual chest measurement	101	119	cm
	40	47	in
Length	56	66	cm
	22	26	in
Sleeve seam	30	38	cm
	12	15	in

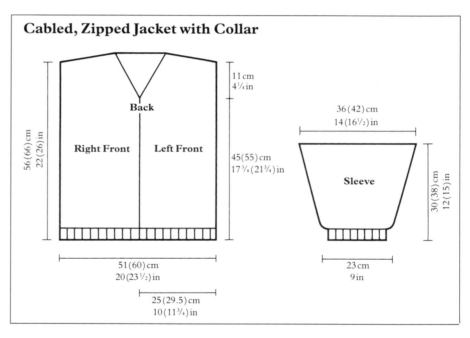

Cabled, Zipped Jacket with Collar

Back

Right Front   Left Front

11 cm
4¼ in

56 (66) cm
22 (26) in

45 (55) cm
17¾ (21¾) in

51 (60) cm
20 (23½) in

25 (29.5) cm
10 (11¾) in

36 (42) cm
14 (16½) in

Sleeve

30 (38) cm
12 (15) in

23 cm
9 in

PANEL B

Worked over 13 sts.

1st row (wrong side) P1, k2, [p1, k1] 3 times, p1, k2, p1.

2nd row K1 tbl, p2, sl next 3 sts onto cable needle and leave at front of work, [k1 tbl, p1] twice, then k1 tbl, p1, k1 tbl from cable needle, p2, k1 tbl.

3rd row As 1st row

4th row K1 tbl, p2, k1 tbl, [p1, k1 tbl] 3 times, p2, k1 tbl.

5th to 10th rows Rep 3rd and 4th rows 3 times.

These 10 rows form patt.

BACK

With 3 ¼mm (No 10/US 3) needles cast on 107 (127) sts.

1st rib row (right side) K1 tbl, [p1, k1 tbl] to end.

2nd rib row P1, [k1, p1] to end.

Rep last 2 rows until welt measures 5cm/2in, ending with a wrong side row.

1st size only

Inc row [Rib 3, m1] twice, rib 2, m1, rib 7, m1, rib 3, m1, rib 2, m1, * rib 2, m1, rib 7, m1, rib 2, m1, rib 3, m1, rib 2, m1, rib 7, m1, rib 3, m1, rib 2, m1; rep from * twice more, rib 3. 137 sts.

Change to 4mm (No 8/US 6) needles.

1st row (wrong side) K2, p1, work 1st row of panel A, [work 1st row of panel B, then panel A] 3 times, p1, k2.

2nd row P2, k1 tbl, work 2nd row of panel A, [work 2nd row of panel B, then panel A] 3 times, k1 tbl, p2.

2nd size only

Inc row Rib 4, *m1, rib 7, [m1, rib 2] twice, m1, rib 3, m1, rib 7, m1, rib 2, m1, rib 3, m1, rib 2; rep from * 3 times more, m1, rib 7, m1, rib 4. (161) sts.

Change to 4mm (No 8/US 6) needles.

1st row (wrong side) K2, work 1st row of panel B, [work 1st row of panel A, then panel B] 4 times, k2.

2nd row P2, work 2nd row of panel B, [work 2nd row of panel A, then panel B] 4 times, p2.

Both sizes

These 2 rows set position of panels. Cont in patt until Back measures 56 (66)cm/22 (26)in from beg, ending with a wrong side row.

Shape Shoulders

Cast off 24 (30) sts at beg of next 4 rows. Cast off rem 41 sts.

LEFT FRONT

With 3 ¼mm (No 10/US 3) needles cast on 52 (62) sts.

1st rib row (right side) K1 tbl, [p1, k1 tbl] to last 3 sts, k3.

2nd rib row K3, p1, [k1, p1] to end.

Rep last 2 rows until welt measures 5cm/2in, ending with a wrong side row.

1st size

Inc row [Rib 3, m1] twice, rib 2, m1, rib 7, m1, rib 3, m1, [rib 2, m1] twice, rib 7, m1, rib 2, m1, rib 3, m1, rib 2, m1, rib 7, m1, rib 3, m1, rib 2, m1, rib 1, k3. 66 sts.

Change to 4mm (No 8/US 6) needles.

1st row (wrong side) K3, p1, work 1st row of panel A, then panel B and panel A, p1, k2.

2nd row P2, k1 tbl, work 2nd row of panel A, then panel B and panel A, k1 tbl, k3.

2nd size

Inc row Rib 2, *rib 2, m1, rib 7, [m1, rib 2] twice, m1, rib 3, m1, rib 7, m1, rib 2, m1, rib 3, m1; rep from * once more, rib 1, k3. (78) sts.

Change to 4mm (No 8/US 6) needles.

1st row (wrong side) K3, p1, [work 1st row of panel A, then panel B] twice, k2.

2nd row P2, [work 2nd row of panel B, then panel A] twice, k1 tbl, k3.

Both sizes

These 2 rows set position of panels. Cont in patt until Front measures 45 (55)cm/17 ¾ (21 ¾)in from beg, end with a wrong side row.

Shape Neck

Next row Patt to last 3 sts, turn; leave the 3 sts on a safety pin.

Keeping patt correct, dec one st at neck edge on next 4 rows, then on every alt row until 48 (60) sts rem. Cont straight until Front matches Back to shoulder shaping, ending with a wrong side row.

Shape Shoulder

Cast off 24 (30) sts at beg of next row. Work 1 row. Cast off rem 24 (30) sts.

RIGHT FRONT

With 3 ¼mm (No 10/US 3) needles cast on 52 (62) sts.

1st rib row (right side) K3, k1 tbl, [p1, k1 tbl] to end.

2nd rib row P1, [k1, p1] to last 3 sts, k3.

Rep last 2 rows until welt measures 5cm/2in, ending with a wrong side row.

1st size

Inc row K3, rib 1, m1, rib 2, m1, rib 3, m1, rib 7, m1, rib 2, m1, rib 3, m1, rib 2, m1, rib 7, m1, [rib 2, m1] twice, rib 3, m1, rib 7, m1, rib 2, [m1, rib 3] twice. 66 sts.

Change to 4mm (No 8/US 6) needles.

1st row (wrong side) K2, p1, work 1st row of panel A, then panel B and panel A, p1, k3.

2nd row K3, k1 tbl, work 2nd row of panel A, then panel B and panel A, k1 tbl, p2.

2nd size

Inc row K3, rib 1, *m1, rib 2, m1, rib 3, m1, rib 7, [m1, rib 2] twice, m1, rib 3, m1, rib 7, m1, rib 2; rep from * once more, rib 2. (78) sts

Change to 4mm (No 8/US 6) needles.

1st row (wrong side) K2, [work 1st row of panel B, then panel A] twice, p1, k3.

2nd row K3, k1 tbl, [work 2nd row of panel A, then panel B] twice, p2.

Both sizes

These 2 rows set position of panels.
Complete as given for Left Front, reversing shapings.

SLEEVES

With 3 ¼mm (No 10/US 3) needles cast on 49 sts.

1st rib row (right side) P1, [k1 tbl, p1] to end.

2nd rib row K1, [p1, k1] to end.

Rep last 2 rows until cuff measures 5cm/2in, ending with a wrong side row.

Inc row Rib 2, m1, rib 3, m1, rib 2, m1, rib 7, m1, rib 3, m1, [rib 2, m1] twice, rib 7, m1, rib 2, m1, rib 3, m1, rib 2, m1, rib 7, m1, rib 3, [m1, rib 2] twice. 63 sts.

Change to 4mm (No 8/US 6) needles.

1st row (wrong side) K1, p1, work 1st row of panel A, then panel B and panel A, p1, k1.

2nd row P1, k1 tbl, work 2nd row of panel A, then panel B and panel A, k1 tbl, p1.

These 2 rows set position of panels. Cont in patt, inc one st at each end of next row and 10 foll 3rd rows, working inc sts into panel B patt. Work in patt, inc one st at each end of 6 (11) foll 4th rows, working inc sts into reverse st st. 97 (107) sts.

Cont straight until Sleeve measures 30 (38)cm/12 (15)in from beg, ending with a wrong side row. Cast off.

COLLAR

Left side

With 4mm (No 8/US 6) needles, rejoin yarn at inside edge to the 3 sts on Left Front safety pin, cast on 4, p1, k2, p1, k3.

Next row K3, k1 tbl, p2, k1 tbl.

Next row Cast on 3, [k1, p1] twice, k2, p1, k3.

Next row K3, k1 tbl, p2, [k1 tbl, p1] twice.

Next row Cast on 3, p1, [k1, p1] 3 times, k2, p1, k3.

Next row K3, k1 tbl, p2, k1 tbl, [p1, k1 tbl] 3 times.

Next row Cast on 3, work 7th row of panel B, k3.

Next row K3, work 8th row of panel B.

Next row Cast on 3, p1, k2 (last 3 sts of 15th row of panel A), work 9th row of panel B, k3.

Next row K3, work 10th row of panel B, p2, k1 tbl (first 3 sts of 16th row of panel A).

Cont in patt, inc one st at inside edge on every row until there are 44 sts, then on 2 foll alt rows, working inc sts into panel A, then panel B. 46 sts.

Work 1 row straight.

Leave these sts on a holder.

Right side

With 4mm (No 8/US 6) needles, rejoin yarn at inside edge to the 3 sts on Right Front safety pin, cast on 4 sts, k1 tbl, p2, k1 tbl, k3.

Next row K3, p1, k2, p1.

Next row Cast on 3 sts, [p1, k1 tbl] twice, p2, k1 tbl, k3.

Next row K3, p1, k2, [p1, k1] twice.

Next row Cast on 3, k1 tbl, [p1, k1 tbl] 3 times, p2, k1 tbl, k3.

Next row K3, p1, k2, p1, [k1, p1] 3 times.

Next row Cast on 3, work 8th row of panel B, k3.

Next row K3, work 9th row of panel B.

Next row Cast on 3, k1 tbl, p2 (last 3 sts of 16th row of panel A), work 10th row of panel B, k3.

Cont in patt, inc one st at inside edge on every row until there are 44 sts, then on 2 foll alt rows, working inc sts into panel A, then panel B. 46 sts.

Work one row.

Next row Patt to end, cast on 35, patt across sts of left side. 127 sts.

Patt 32 rows.

Next row Patt 17 sts and sl these sts onto a holder, patt to last 17 sts, turn; leave the last 17 sts on a holder.

Work on center 93 sts only. Keeping patt correct, dec one st at each end of next 5 rows. Cast off 3 sts at beg of next 4 rows, 4 sts at beg of foll 4 rows and 5 sts at beg of foll 8 rows.

Cast off rem 15 sts.

Rejoin yarn at inside edge to one set of 17 sts and cont in patt until border fits round shaped edge of collar to center. Leave these sts. Work other side to match. With right sides of border together, cast off together border sts.

TO MAKE UP

Join shoulder seams. Sew collar border in place, then sew on collar. Sew on sleeves, placing center of sleeves to shoulder seams. Join side and sleeve seams. Sew in zip fastener.

Ribbed Denim Sweater

MATERIALS
12 (14: 15: 17: 19) 50g balls of Rowan Denim.
Pair each of 3 ¼mm (No 10/US 3), 3 ¾mm (No 9/US 4) and 4mm (No 8/US 6) knitting needles.

TENSION
20 sts and 30 rows to 10cm/4in square over rib pattern on 4mm (No 8/US 6) needles.

ABBREVIATIONS
See page 8.

BACK
With 3 ¾mm (No9/US 4) needles cast on 82 (87: 97: 102: 112) sts.
1st rib row (right side) K2, [p3, k2] to end.
2nd rib row P.
These two rows form rib patt. Rep last 2 rows once more.
Change to 4mm (No 8/US 6) needles.
Cont in patt until Back measures 31 (35: 38: 41: 46)cm/12 (13 ¾: 15: 16: 18)in from beg. Mark each end of last row.
Cast on one st at beg of next 2 rows. 84 (89: 99: 104: 114) sts.
Cont in patt until Back measures 50 (55: 60: 65: 71)cm/19 ½ (21 ½: 23 ½: 25 ½: 28)in from beg, ending with a right side row.

Shape Neck
Next row Patt 33 (34: 39: 42: 47), turn.
Work on this set of sts only. Keeping patt correct, cast off 2 (2: 3: 3: 4) sts at beg of next row and foll alt row. 29 (30: 33: 36: 39) sts.

Shape Shoulder
Cast off 10 (10: 11: 12: 13) sts at beg of next row and foll alt row. Work 1 row. Cast off rem 9 (10: 11: 12: 13) sts.
With wrong side facing, slip center 18 (21: 21: 20: 20) sts onto a holder, rejoin yarn to rem sts, cast off 2 (2: 3: 3: 4) sts, patt to end. Patt 1 row. Cast off 2 (2: 3: 3: 4) sts at beg of next row.

Shape Shoulder
Cast off 10 (10: 11: 12: 13) sts at beg of next row and foll alt row. Work 1 row. Cast off rem 9 (10: 11: 12: 13) sts.

MEASUREMENTS

To fit age	3-4	4-6	6–8	8-9	9-10	years

The following measurements are after the garment has been washed to the instructions given on the ball band.

	3-4	4-6	6–8	8-9	9-10	
Actual chest	82	87	97	102	112	cm
measurement	32	34	38	40	44	in
Length	44	48	53	57	62	cm
	17 ¼	19	21	22 ½	24 ½	in
Sleeve seam	28	30	35	38	43	cm
	11	12	13 ¾	15	17	in

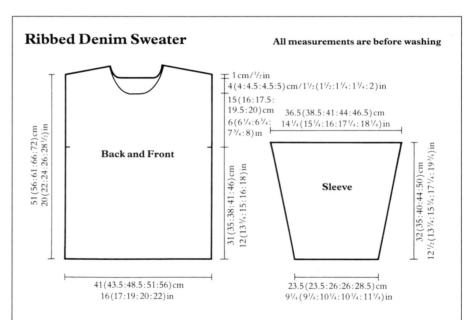

Ribbed Denim Sweater   All measurements are before washing

Back and Front

51(56:61:66:72)cm
20(22:24:26:28½)in

41(43.5:48.5:51:56)cm
16(17:19:20:22)in

1 cm/½in
4(4:4.5:4.5:5)cm/1½(1½:1¾:1¾:2)in
15(16:17.5:19.5:20)cm
6(6¼:6¾:7¾:8)in
36.5(38.5:41:44:46.5)cm
14¼(15¼:16:17¼:18¼)in

31(35:38:41:46)cm
12(13¾:15:16:18)in

Sleeve

32(35:40:44:50)cm
12½(13¾:15¾:17¼:19½)in

23.5(23.5:26:26:28.5)cm
9¼(9¼:10¼:10¼:11¼)in

FRONT
Work as given for Back until Front measures 46 (51: 55.5: 60.5: 66)cm/18 (20: 21 ¾: 23 ¾: 26)in from beg, ending with a right side row.

Shape Neck
Next row Patt 35 (36: 40: 43: 47), turn. Work on this set of sts only. Dec one st at neck edge on next 3 rows, then on 3 (3: 4: 4: 5) foll alt rows. 29 (30: 33: 36: 39) sts. Cont straight until Front matches Back to shoulder shaping, ending at side edge.

Shape Shoulder
Cast off 10 (10: 11: 12: 13) sts at beg of next row and foll alt row. Work 1 row. Cast off rem 9 (10: 11: 12: 13) sts.
With wrong side facing, slip center 14 (17: 19: 18: 20) sts onto a holder, rejoin yarn to rem sts and patt to end. Complete as given for first side.

SLEEVES
With 3 ¾mm (No 9/US 4) needles cast on 47 (47: 52: 52: 57) sts.
Work in rib patt as given for Back for 6cm/ 2 ½in.
Change to 4mm (No 8/US 6) needles.
Cont in patt, inc one st at each end of 5th row and every foll 5th (5th: 6th: 5th: 6th) row until there are 73 (77: 82: 88: 93) sts, working inc sts into patt.
Cont straight until Sleeve measures 32 (35: 40: 44: 50)cm/12 ½(13 ¾: 15 ¾: 17 ¼: 19 ¾)in from beg, ending with a wrong side row.
Cast off.

NECKBAND
Join right shoulder seam.
With 3 ¼mm (No 10/US 3) needles and right side facing, k up 16 (16: 18: 18: 20) sts down left front neck, k center front sts, k up 16 (16: 18: 18: 20) sts up right front neck, 9 (9: 10: 11: 13) sts down right back neck, k center back sts, k up 9 (9: 10: 11: 13) sts up left back neck. 82 (88: 96: 96: 106) sts.
Work 9 (9: 11: 13: 13) rows in k1, p1 rib.
Beg with a k row, work 8 (8: 10: 10: 12) rows in st st.
Cast off loosely.

TO MAKE UP
Join left shoulder and neckband seam, reversing seam on st st section of neckband. Sew on sleeves between markers. Join side and sleeve seams.

Right: Cream Denim Sweater (see page 27) and Ribbed Denim Sweater.

Cream Denim Sweater

MATERIALS
16 (17: 18) 50g balls of Rowan Denim.
Pair each of 3 ¼mm (No 10/US 3), 3 ¾mm
(No 9/US 4) and 4mm (No 8/US 6)
knitting needles.
Cable needle.

TENSION
21 sts and 30 rows to 10cm/4in square
over moss st on 4mm (No 8/US 6) needles
before washing.

ABBREVIATIONS
C2B = sl next st onto cable needle and leave
at back of work, k1, then k1 from cable
needle;
C2F = sl next st onto cable needle and leave
at front of work, k1, then k1 from cable
needle;
C3B = sl next st onto cable needle and leave
at back of work, k2, then k1 from cable
needle;
C3F = sl next 2 sts onto cable needle and
leave at front of work, k1, then k2 from
cable needle;
C6F = sl next 3 sts onto cable needle and
leave at front of work, k3, then k3 from
cable needle;
Cr2L = sl next st onto cable needle and
leave at front of work, p1, then k1 from
cable needle;
Cr2R = sl next st onto cable needle and
leave at back of work, k1, then p1 from
cable needle;
Cr3L = sl next 2 sts onto cable needle and
leave at front of work, p1, then k2 from
cable needle;
Cr3R = sl next st onto cable needle and
leave at back of work, k2, then p1 from
cable needle;
Also see page 8.

MEASUREMENTS

To fit age	4-6	6–8	8-10	years

The following measurements are after the garment has been washed to the instructions given on ball band.

Actual chest	104	118	124	cm
measurement	41	46 ½	49	in
Length	51	56	61	cm
	20	22	24	in
Sleeve seam	29	33	39	cm
	11 ½	13	15 ½	in

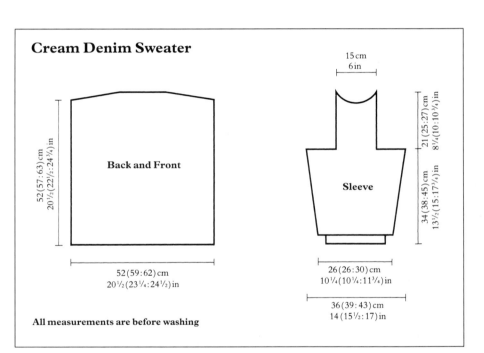

Cream Denim Sweater

Back and Front

52(57:63)cm
20½(22½:24¾)in

52(59:62)cm
20½(23¼:24½)in

15cm
6in

Sleeve

21(25:27)cm
8¼(10:10¾)in

34(38:45)cm
13½(15:17¾)in

26(26:30)cm
10¼(10¼:11¾)in

36(39:43)cm
14(15½:17)in

All measurements are before washing

PANEL A
Worked over 8 sts.
1st row (right side) K6, p1, k1.
2nd row P2, k1, p5.
3rd row K4, [p1, k1] twice.
4th row P2, k1, p1, k1 p3.
5th row K2, [p1, k1] 3 times.
6th row P2, [k1, p1] 3 times.
7th row As 5th row.
8th row As 4th row.
9th row As 3rd row.
10th row As 2nd row.
These 10 rows form patt.

PANEL B
Worked over 18 sts.
1st row (right side) P5, k8, p5.
2nd row K5, p8, k5.
3rd row P4, Cr2R, k6, Cr2L, p4.
4th row K4, p1, k1, p6, k1, p1, k4.
5th row P3, Cr2R, p1, k6, p1, Cr2L, p3.
6th row K3, p1, k2, p6, k2, p1, k3.
7th row P2, Cr2R, p2, C6F, p2, Cr2L, p2.
8th row K2, p1, k3, p6, k3, p1, k2.
9th row P1, Cr2R, p3, k6, p3, Cr2L, p1.
10th row K1, p1, k4, p6, k4, p1, k1.
11th row P1, Cr2L, p3, k6, p3, Cr2R, p1.
12th row As 8th row.
13th row P2, Cr2L, p2, C6F, p2, Cr2R, p2.
14th row As 6th row.
15th row P3, Cr2L, p1, k6, p1, Cr2R, p3.
16th row As 4th row.
17th row P4, Cr2L, k6, Cr2R, p4.
18th row K5, p8, k5.
Rows 3 to 18 form patt.

PANEL C
Worked over 8 sts.
1st row (right side) K1, p1, k6.
2nd row P5, k1, p2.
3rd row [K1, p1] twice, k4.
4th row P3, k1, p1, k1, p2.
5th row [K1, p1] 3 times, k2.
6th row [P1, k1] 3 times, p2.
7th row As 5th row.
8th row As 4th row.
9th row As 3rd row.
10th row As 2nd row.
These 10 rows form patt.

PANEL D
Worked over 14 sts.
1st row (right side) P3, k8, p3.
2nd row K3, p8, k3.
3rd row P4, C3B, Cr3L, p4.
4th row K4, p3, k1, p2, k4.
5th row P3, Cr3R, k1, p1, C3F, p3.
6th row K3, p2, [k1, p1] twice, p2, k3.
7th row P2, C3B, [p1, k1] twice, Cr3L, p2.
8th row K2, p3, [k1, p1] twice, k1, p2, k2.
9th row P1, Cr3R, [k1, p1] 3 times, C3F, p1.
10th row K1, p2, [k1, p1] 4 times, p2, k1.
11th row P1, Cr3L, [k1, p1] 3 times, Cr3R, p1.
12th row As 8th row.
13th row P2, Cr3L, [p1, k1] twice, Cr3R, p2.
14th row As 6th row.
15th row P3, Cr3L, k1, p1, Cr3R, p3.
16th row As 4th row.
17th row P4, Cr3L, Cr3R, p4.
18th row K5, p4, k5.
19th row P3, sl next 2 sts onto cable needle and leave at back of work, k2, then k2 from cable needle, sl next 2 sts onto cable needle and leave at front of work, k2, then k2 from cable needle, p3.
20th row K3, p8, k3.
21st row P3, k8, p3.
22nd row As 20th row.
23rd and 24th rows As 19th and 20th rows.
These 24 rows form patt.

BACK AND FRONT ALIKE
With 3 ¾mm (No 9/US 4) needles, cast on 116 (128: 140) sts.
1st row (right side) K41 (47: 53), work 1st row of panels A, B and C, k to end.
2nd row P2, [k2, p4] 6 (7: 8) times, k2, p1, work 2nd row of panels C, B and A, [k2, p4] 6 (7: 8) times, k2, p3.
3rd row K2, [C2F, k4] 6 (7: 8) times, C2F, k1, patt 34 sts as set, [C2F, k4] 6 (7: 8) times, C2F, k3.
4th row P2, [k1, p1, k1, p3] 6 (7: 8) times, k1, p1, k1, patt 34, [k1, p1, k1, p3] 6 (7: 8) times, k1, p1, k1, p2.
5th row K3, [C2F, k4] 6 (7: 8) times, C2F, patt 34, k1, [C2F, k4] 6 (7: 8) times, C2F, k2.
6th row P3, [k2, p4] 6 (7: 8) times, k2, patt 34, p1, [k2, p4] 6 (7: 8) times, k2, p2.
7th row K41 (47: 53), patt 34, k to end.
8th row As 6th row.
9th row K3, [C2B, k4] 6 (7: 8) times, C2B, patt 34, k1, [C2B, k4] 6 (7: 8) times, C2B, k2.
10th row As 4th row.
11th row K2, [C2B, k4] 6 (7: 8) times, C2B, k1, patt 34, [C2B, k4] 6 (7: 8) times, C2B, k3.
12th row P2, [k2, p4] 6 (7: 8) times, k2, p1, patt 34, [k2, p4] 6 (7: 8) times, k2, p3.
Work a further 37 rows as set.
Inc row [Patt 8 (9: 16), m1] 5 (5: 3) times, patt 36 (38: 44), [m1, patt 8 (9: 16)] 5 (5: 3) times. 126 (138: 146) sts.
Change to 4mm (No 8/US 6) needles.
1st row (right side) [K1, p1] 3 (2: 4) times, [work 1st row of panel A] 0 (1: 1) time, [work 3rd row of panel B, work 1st row of panels C, D and A] twice, work 3rd row of panel B, [work 1st row of panel C] 0 (1: 1) time, [p1, k1] 3 (2: 4) times.
2nd row [K1, p1] 3 (2: 4) times, [work 2nd row of panel C] 0 (1: 1) time, [work 4th row of panel B, work 2nd row of panel A, D and C] twice, work 4th row of panel B, [work 2nd row of panel A] 0 (1: 1) time, [p1, k1] 3 (2: 4) times.
These 2 rows set position of panels.
Cont in patt until work measures 52 (57: 63)cm/20 ½ (22 ½: 24 ¾)in from beg, ending with a wrong side row.

Shape Shoulders
Cast off 15 (17: 18) sts at beg of next 4 rows and 15 (17: 19) sts at beg of foll 2 rows.
Leave rem 36 sts on a holder.

SLEEVES

With 3 ¼mm (No 10/US 3) needles cast on 43 (43: 49) sts.

1st row (right side) K.

2nd row P2, [k2, p4] to last 5 sts, k2, p3.

3rd row K2, [C2F, k4] to last 5 sts, C2F, k3.

4th row P2, [k1, p1, k1, p3] to last 5 sts, k1, p1, k1, p2.

5th row K3, [C2F, k4] to last 4 sts, C2F, k2.

6th row P3, [k2, p4] to last 4 sts, k2, p2.

7th row K.

8th row As 6th row.

9th row K3, [C2B, k4] to last 4 sts, C2B, k2.

10th row As 4th row.

11th row K2, [C2B, k4] to last 5 sts, C2B, k3.

12th row As 2nd row.

Work a further 5 rows as set.

Inc row Patt 1 (1: 3), [m1, rib 2] to end. 64 (64: 72) sts.

Change to 4mm (No 8/US 6) needles.

1st row Work last 1 (1: 5) sts of 1st row of panel C, work 1st row of panels D, A, B, C and D, work first 1 (1: 5) sts of 1st row of panel A.

2nd row Work last 1 (1: 5) sts of 2nd row of panel A, work 2nd row of panels D, C, B, A and D, work first 1 (1: 5) sts of 2nd row of panel C.

These 2 rows set position of panels.

Cont in patt, inc one st at each end of 7th row and every foll 6th (6th: 7th) row until there are 84 (92: 98) sts, working inc sts into panel A and C as set, then into moss st. Cont straight until Sleeve measures 34 (38: 45)cm/13 ½ (15: 17 ¾)in from beg, ending with a wrong side row.

Shape Saddle

Cast off 24 (28: 31) sts at beg of next 2 rows.

Patt a further 18 (22: 24)cm/7 (8 ¾: 9 ½)in on rem 36 sts.

Shape Neck

Next row Patt 8, work 2 tog, turn.

Work on this set of sts only. Dec one st at inside edge on every row until 2 sts rem. Work 2 tog and fasten off.

With right side facing, slip center 16 sts onto a holder, rejoin yarn, work 2 tog and patt to end. Complete as given for first side.

NECKBAND

With 3 ¼mm (No 10/US 3) needles and right side facing, k up 10 sts down first side of left sleeve, k center sleeve sts, k up 10 sts up second side of left sleeve, patt across center front sts, k up 10 sts down first side of right sleeve, k center sleeve sts, k up 9 sts up second side of right sleeve, k center back sts. 143 sts.

Next row P1, *patt 34, p2, [k2, p4] 5 times, k2, p3; rep from * once more.

Next row * K2, C2F, [k4, C2F] 5 times, k3, patt 34; rep from * once more, k1.

Patt a further 13 rows as set.

Next row K2, [k2 tog, k4] to last 3 sts, k2 tog, k1. 119 sts.

Beg with a p row, work 9 rows in st st.

Cast off loosely.

TO MAKE UP

Wash garment according to the instructions given on the ball band. Join neckband seam, reversing seam on st st section. Sew saddles to shoulders. Sew on remainder of sleeves in place. Join side and sleeve seams.

Denim Fisherman Shirt

MATERIALS
13 (15: 17: 19) 50g balls of Rowan Denim.
Pair each of 3 ¼mm (No 10/US 3), 3 ¾mm
(No 9/US 4) and 4mm (No 8/US 6)
knitting needles.
Cable needle.

TENSION
20 sts and 28 rows to 10cm/4in square over
st st on 4mm (No 8/US 6) needles before
washing.

ABBREVIATIONS
C2B = sl next st onto cable needle and leave
at back of work, k1, then k1 tbl from cable
needle;
C2F = sl next st onto cable needle and leave
at front of work, k1 tbl, then k1 from cable
needle;
Cr2L = sl next st onto cable needle and
leave at front of work, p1, then k1 from
cable needle;
Cr2R = sl next st onto cable needle and
leave at back of work, k1, then p1 from
cable needle;
mb = [k1, p1, k1, p1, k1] all in next st, turn,
p5, turn, k5, turn, p2 tog, p1, p2 tog tbl,
turn, k3 tog.
Also see page 8.

PANEL A
Worked over 9sts.
1st row (right side) P2, Cr2R, k1 tbl,
Cr2L, p2.
2nd row K2, p1, [k1, p1] twice, k2.
3rd row P1, C2B, p1, k1 tbl, p1, C2F, p1.
4th row K1, p2, k1, p1, k1, p2, k1.
5th row Cr2R, k1 tbl, [p1, k1 tbl] twice,
Cr2L.
6th row P1, [k1, p1] 4 times.
7th row Cr2L, k1 tbl, [p1, k1 tbl] twice,
Cr2R.
8th row As 4th row.
9th row P1, Cr2L, p1, k1 tbl, p1, Cr2R, p1.
10th row As 2nd row.
11th row P2, Cr2L, k1 tbl, Cr2R, p2.
12th row K3, p3, k3.
13th row P3, sl next 2 sts onto cable needle
and leave at back of work, k1, then k1 tbl, k1
from cable needle, p3.
14th row K3, p3, k3.
These 14 rows form patt.

MEASUREMENTS

To fit age	3-5	6-7	7–8	9-10	years

The following measurements are after the garment has been washed to the instructions given on the ball band.

	3-5	6-7	7–8	9-10	
Actual chest	96	104	116	124	cm
measurement	38	41	45 ½	49	in
Length	44	48	53	58	cm
	17 ½	19	21	23	in
Sleeve seam	26	32	36	40	cm
	10 ¼	12 ½	14 ¼	15 ¾	in

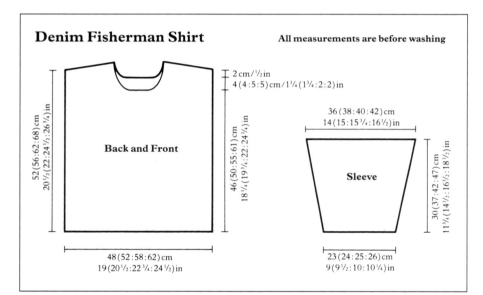

Denim Fisherman Shirt All measurements are before washing

Back and Front

52 (56:62:68) cm
20½ (22:24½:26¾) in

46 (50:55:61) cm
18¼ (19¾:22:24¼) in

48 (52:58:62) cm
19 (20½:22¾:24½) in

2 cm/½ in
4 (4:5:5) cm/1¼ (1¼:2:2) in

36 (38:40:42) cm
14 (15:15¾:16½) in

Sleeve

30 (37:42:47) cm
11¾ (14½:16½:18½) in

23 (24:25:26) cm
9 (9½:10:10¼) in

PANEL B

Worked over 9 sts.

1st row (right side) Sl next st onto cable needle and leave at back of work, k1 tbl, then k1 from cable needle, p7.

2nd row K6, Cr2L, p1.

3rd row K1 tbl, p1, C2F, p5.

4th row K4, Cr2L, p1, k1, p1.

5th row [K1 tbl, p1] twice, C2F, p3.

6th row K2, Cr2L, [p1, k1] twice, p1.

7th row [K1 tbl, p1] 3 times, C2F, p1.

8th row Cr2L, [p1, k1] 3 times, p1.

9th row [K1 tbl, p1] 4 times, k1 tbl.

10th row P1, [k1, p1] 3 times, Cr2L.

11th row P1, Cr2L, [p1, k1 tbl] 3 times.

12th row P1, [k1, p1] twice, Cr2L, k2.

13th row P3, Cr2L, [p1, k1 tbl] twice.

14th row P1, k1, p1, Cr2L, k4.

15th row P5, Cr2L, p1, k1 tbl.

16th row P1, Cr2L, k6.

17th row P7, sl next st onto cable needle and leave at front of work, k1, then k1 tbl from cable needle.

18th row P1, Cr2R, k6.

19th row P5, C2B, p1, k1 tbl.

20th row P1, k1, p1, Cr2R, k4.

21st row P3, C2B, [p1, k1 tbl] twice.

22nd row P1, [k1, p1] twice, Cr2R, k2.

23rd row P1, C2B, [p1, k1 tbl] 3 times.

24th row P1, [k1, p1] 3 times, Cr2R.

25th row K1 tbl, [p1, k1 tbl] 4 times.

26th row Cr2R, [p1, k1] 3 times, p1.

27th row [K1 tbl, p1] 3 times, Cr2R, p1.

28th row K2, Cr2R, [p1, k1] twice, p1.

29th row [K1 tbl, p1] twice, Cr2R, p3.

30th row K4, Cr2R, p1, k1, p1.

31st row K1 tbl, p1, Cr2R, p5.

32nd row K6, Cr2R, p1.

These 32 rows form patt.

PANEL C

Rep of 11 sts.

1st row (right side) *P3, Cr2R, k1, Cr2L, p3; rep from *.

2nd row *K3, p1, [k1, p1] twice, k3; rep from *.

3rd row *P2, Cr2R, k1, p1, k1, Cr2L, p2; rep from *.

4th row *K2, p1, [k1, p1] 3 times, k2; rep from *.

5th row *P1, Cr2R, k1, [p1, k1] twice, Cr2L, p1; rep from *.

6th row *K1, [p1, k1] 5 times; rep from *.

7th row *Cr2R, k1, [p1, k1] 3 times, Cr2L; rep from *.

8th row *P1, [k1, p1] 5 times; rep from *.

9th row *Cr2L, p1, [k1, p1] 3 times, Cr2R; rep from *.

10th row As 6th row.

11th row *P1, Cr2L, p1, [k1, p1] twice, Cr2R, p1; rep from *.

12th row As 4th row.

13th row *P2, Cr2L, p1, k1, p1, Cr2R, p2; rep from *.

14th row As 2nd row.

15th row *P3, Cr2L, p1, Cr2R, p3; rep from *.

16th row *K4, p1, k1, p1, k4; rep from *.

17th row P4, *sl next 2 sts onto cable needle and leave at back of work, k1, then p1, k1 from cable needle**, p4, pick up loop lying between st just worked and next st and work into back, front, back and front of the loop, then pass 2nd, 3rd, and 4th st over first st, p next st, then pass bobble st over the p st, p3***; rep from * to *** to last 7 sts, rep from * to **, p4.

18th row As 16th row.

These 18 rows form patt.

BACK

With 3 ¾mm (No 9/US 4) needles cast on 113 (125: 137: 149) sts.

1st row (right side) P1, k3, *p2, Cr2R, k1, Cr2L, p2, k3; rep from * to last st, p1.

2nd row K1, p3, *k2, p1, [k1, p1] twice, k2, p3; rep from * to last st, k1.

3rd row P1, k3, *p1, Cr2R, p1, k1, p1, Cr2L, p1, k3; rep from * to last st, p1.

4th row K1, p3, *k1, p1, [k2, p1] twice, k1, p3; rep from * to last st, k1.

5th row P1, k3, *Cr2R, p2, k1, p2, Cr2L, k3; rep from * to last st, p1.

6th row K1, p3, *k4, p1, k4, p3; rep from * to last st, k1.

These 6 rows form welt patt.

Rep last 6 rows 10 (11: 12: 13) times more, dec one st at center on 2nd and 4th sizes only. 113 (124: 137: 148) sts.

Change to 4mm (No 8/US 6) needles.

1st row (right side) P1, [k3, welt patt 9 sts] 0 (0: 1: 1) time, k3, work 1st row of panel A, k3, work 1st row of panel B, k3, welt patt 9 sts, k3, work 1st row of panel C across next 33 (44: 33: 44) sts, k3, welt patt 9 sts, k3, work 17th row of panel B, k3, work 1st row of panel A, k3, [welt patt 9 sts, k3] 0 (0: 1: 1) time, p1.

2nd row K1, [p3, welt patt 9 sts] 0 (0: 1: 1) time, p3, work 2nd row of panel A, p3, work 18th row of panel B, p3, welt patt 9 sts, p3, work 2nd row of panel C across next 33 (44: 33: 44) sts, p3, welt patt 9, p3, work 2nd row of panel B, p3, work 2nd row of panel A, p3, [welt patt 9, p3] 0 (0: 1: 1) time, k1.

3rd row P1, [k1, mb, k1, welt patt 9 sts] 0 (0: 1: 1) time, k1, mb, k1, work 3rd row of panel A, k1, mb, k1, work 3rd row of panel B, k1, mb, k1, welt patt 9 sts, k1, mb, k1, work 3rd row of panel C across next 33 (44: 33: 44) sts, k1, mb, k1, welt patt 9 sts, k1, mb, k1, work 19th row of panel B, k1, mb, k1, work 3rd row of panel A, k1, mb, k1, [welt patt 9 sts, k1, mb, k1] 0 (0: 1: 1) time, p1.

F

MA
8 (9
Ha
2 b
Pai
4m

TE
21
pat

AE
See

BA
Wit
cas
1st
2nd
Th
2cr
Ch
Co
18:
fro
Ch
Ch
Ch
row
Co
53:
fro

Sh
Ca:
2 r
foll
on :

4th row K1, [p3, welt patt 9 sts] 0 (0: 1: 1) time, p3, work 4th row of panel A, p3, work 20th row of panel B, p3, welt patt 9 sts, p3, work 4th row of panel C across next 33 (44: 33: 44) sts, p3, welt patt 9 sts, p3, work 4th row of panel B, p3, work 4th row of panel A, p3, [welt patt 9 sts, p3] 0 (0: 1: 1) time, k1.
5th row P1, [k3, welt patt 9 sts] 0 (0: 1: 1) time, k3, work 5th row of panel A, k3, work 5th row of panel B, k3, welt patt 9 sts, k3, work 5th row of panel C across next 33 (44: 33: 44) sts, k3, welt patt 9 sts, k3, work 21st row of panel B, k3, work 5th row of panel A, k3, [welt patt 9 sts, k3] 0 (0: 1: 1) time, p1.
6th row K1, [p3, welt patt 9 sts] 0 (0: 1: 1) time, p3, work 6th row of panel A, p3, work 22nd row of panel B, p3, welt patt 9 sts, p3, work 6th row of panel C across next 33 (44: 33: 44) sts, p3, welt patt 9 sts, p3, work 6th row of panel B, p3, work 6th row of panel A, p3, [welt patt 9 sts, p3] 0 (0: 1: 1) time, k1.
These six rows set position of panels and form bobble patt between panels.
Cont in patt until Back measures 50 (54: 60: 66)cm/20 (21 ½: 24: 26 ¼)in from beg, ending with a wrong side row.

Shape Neck
Next row Patt 43 (48: 54: 59), turn.
Work on this set of sts only. Keeping patt correct, cast off 3 sts at beg of next row and foll alt row.

Shape Shoulder
Cast off 12 (14: 16: 18) sts at beg of next row and foll alt row. Work 1 row. Cast off rem 13 (14: 16: 17) sts.
With right side facing, slip center 27 (28: 29: 30) sts onto a holder, rejoin yarn to rem sts, patt to end. Patt 1 row. Complete to match first side.

FRONT
Work as given for Back until Front measures 46 (50: 55: 61)cm/18 ¼ (19 ¾: 22: 24 ¼)in from beg, ending with a wrong side row.

Shape Neck
Next row Patt 45 (50: 56: 61), turn.
Work on this set of sts only. Dec one st at neck edge on next 8 rows. 37 (42: 48: 53) sts.
Cont straight until Front matches Back to shoulder shaping, ending at side edge.

Shape Shoulder
Cast off 12 (14: 16: 18) sts at beg of next row and foll alt row. Work 1 row. Cast off rem 13 (14: 16: 17) sts.
With right side facing, slip center 23 (24: 25: 26) sts onto a holder, rejoin yarn to rem sts, patt to end. Complete to match first side.

SLEEVES
With 3 ¼mm (No 10/US 3) needles, cast on 57 (59: 61: 63) sts.
1st row (right side) K0 (1: 2: 3), p2, Cr2R, k1, Cr2L, p2, *k3, p2, Cr2R, k1, Cr2L, p2; rep from * to last 0 (1: 2: 3) sts, k0 (1: 2: 3).
2nd row P0 (1: 2: 3), k2, p1, [k1, p1] twice, k2, *p3, k2, p1, [k1, p1] twice, k2; rep from * to last 0 (1: 2: 3) sts, p0 (1: 2: 3).
These 2 rows set welt patt.
Patt a further 16 rows.
Change to 4mm (No 8/US 6) needles.
1st row (right side) K0 (1: 2: 3), welt patt 9 sts, k3, work 1st row of panel C across next 33 sts, k3, welt patt 9 sts, k0 (1: 2: 3).
2nd row P0 (1: 2: 3), welt patt 9 sts, p3, work 2nd row of panel C across next 33 sts, p3, welt patt 9, p0 (1: 2: 3).
These 2 rows set position of panels.
Cont in patt, inc one st at each end of next row and every foll 4th (5th: 5th: 6th) row until there are 85 (89: 93: 97) sts, working inc sts into bobble patt then into moss st (k the p sts and p the k sts).
Cont straight until Sleeve measures 30 (37: 42: 47)cm/11 ¾ (14 ½: 16 ½: 18 ½)in from beg, ending with a wrong side row.
Cast off.

NECKBAND
Join right shoulder seam.
With 3 ¼mm (No 10/US 3) needles and right side facing, k up 14 (14: 17: 17) sts down left front neck, k center front sts, k up 14 (14: 17: 17) sts up right front neck, k up 8 sts down right back neck, k center back sts, k up 8 sts up left back neck. 94 (96: 104: 106) sts.
Beg with a p row, work 15 rows in st st. Cast off loosely.

TO MAKE UP
Wash garment according to the instructions given on the ball band. Join left shoulder and neckband seam, reversing seam on last 6 rows of neckband. Sew on sleeves, placing center of sleeves to shoulder seams. Join side and sleeve seams.

FRONT

Work as given for Back until Front is 12 (14: 16: 16: 18) rows less than Back to shoulder shaping, ending with a wrong side row.

Shape Neck

Next row Patt 37 (39: 41: 46: 50) turn. Work on this set of sts only.
Keeping patt correct, dec one st at neck edge on every row until 29 (31: 33: 38: 42) sts rem. Patt 3 (5: 7: 7: 9) rows straight.

Shape Shoulder

Cast off 15 (15: 17: 19: 21) sts at beg of next row. Patt 1 row.
Cast off rem 14 (16: 16: 19: 21) sts.
With right side facing, slip center 14 (15: 16: 16: 18) sts onto a holder, rejoin yarn to rem sts and patt to end. Complete to match first side, but working 1 row more before shaping shoulder.

SLEEVES

With 3 ¼mm (No 10/US 3) needles and A, cast on 43 (43: 48: 48: 53) sts.
Work 2cm/¾in in patt as given for Back.
Change to 4mm (No 8/US 6) needles.
Work 7 rows in patt, inc one st at each end of 3rd row and foll 4th row.
Change to B and patt 4 rows, inc one st at each end of 4th row.
Change to A and patt 4 rows, inc one st at each end of 4th row.
Change to B and patt 4 rows, inc one st at each end of 4th row.
Cont in A only, inc one st at each end of every foll 4th row until there are 75 (83: 88: 94: 97) sts.
Cont straight until Sleeve measures 28 (31: 35: 38: 41)cm/11 (12 ¼: 13 ¾: 15: 16)in from beg, ending with a wrong side row.
Cast off.

NECKBAND

Join right shoulder seam.
With 3 ¼mm (No 10/US 3) needles, A and right side facing, k up 19 (18: 21: 21: 25) sts down left front neck, patt center front sts, k up 18 (17: 21: 21: 24) sts up right front neck, patt back neck sts, dec one st at end on 1st and 5th sizes only. 80 (81: 90: 90: 100) sts.
1st rib row P3 (2: 0: 0: 0), [k2, p3] to last 2 (4: 0: 0: 0) sts, k2 (2: 0: 0: 0), p0 (2: 0: 0: 0).
2nd rib row K0 (2: 0: 0: 0), p2 (2: 0: 0: 0), [k3, p2] to last 3 (2: 0: 0: 0) sts, k3 (2: 0: 0: 0).
Rep last 2 rows 4 (4: 5: 5: 6) times more, then work 1st row again. Working k for p and p for k on next row (thus reversing fabric), rib 11 (11: 13: 13: 15) rows. Cast off loosely in rib.

TO MAKE UP

Join left shoulder and neckband seam, reversing seam on reversed part of neckband.
Sew on sleeves, placing center of sleeves to shoulder seams. Join side and sleeve seams.

Stocking-stitch Sweater with Collar

MATERIALS

5 (5: 6: 7: 7) 50g balls of Rowan True 4 ply Botany.
Pair each of 2 ¾mm (No 12/US 2) and 3 ¼mm (No 10/US 3) knitting needles.
Set of four 2 ¾mm (No 12/US 2) double pointed knitting needles.

TENSION

28 sts and 36 rows to 10cm/4in square over st st on 3 ¼mm (No 10/US 3) needles.

ABBREVIATIONS

See page 8.

BACK

With 2 ¾mm (No 12/US 2) needles cast on 98 (114: 126: 140: 154) sts.
K 7 rows.
Change to 3 ¼mm (No 10/US 3) needles.
Next row (right side) K.
Next row K5, p to last 5 sts, k5.
Rep last 2 rows 3 times more.
Beg with a k row, work in st st until Back measures 38 (45: 50: 55: 60)cm/15 (17 ¾: 19 ¾: 21 ¾: 23 ¾)in from beg, ending with a p row.

Shape Shoulders

Cast off 14 (17: 20: 23: 26) sts at beg of next 2 rows and 14 (18: 20: 23: 26) sts at beg of foll 2 rows. Leave rem 42 (44: 46: 48: 50) sts on a holder.

MEASUREMENTS

To fit age	1-2	3-4	4-6	6–8	8-10	years
Actual chest	70	81	90	100	110	cm
measurement	27 ½	32	35 ½	39 ½	43	in
Length	38	45	50	55	60	cm
	15	17 ¾	19 ¾	21 ¾	23 ¾	in
Sleeve seam	23	27	30	35	40	cm
	9	10 ½	11 ¾	13 ¾	15 ¾	in

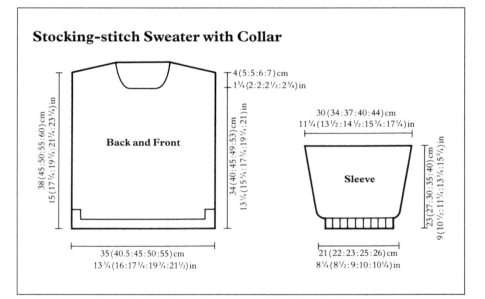

Stocking-stitch Sweater with Collar

Back and Front

38 (45: 50: 55: 60) cm
15 (17 ¾: 19 ¾: 21 ¾: 23 ¾) in

34 (40: 45: 49: 53) cm
13 ¼ (15 ¾: 17 ¾: 19 ¼: 21) in

35 (40.5: 45: 50: 55) cm
13 ¾ (16: 17 ¾: 19 ¾: 21 ½) in

4 (5: 5: 6: 7) cm
1 ¾ (2: 2: 2 ½: 2 ¾) in

Sleeve

30 (34: 37: 40: 44) cm
11 ¾ (13 ½: 14 ½: 15 ¾: 17 ¼) in

23 (27: 30: 35: 40) cm
9 (10 ½: 11 ¾: 13 ¾: 15 ¾) in

21 (22: 23: 25: 26) cm
8 ¼ (8 ½: 9: 10: 10 ¼) in

FRONT

Work as given for Back until Front measures 34 (40: 45: 49: 53)cm/13 ¼ (15 ¾: 17 ¾: 19 ¼: 21)in from beg, ending with a p row.

Shape Neck

Next row K35 (43: 48: 55: 62), turn.
Work on this set of sts only. Dec one st at neck edge on every row until 28 (35: 40: 46: 52) sts rem.
Cont straight until Front matches Back to shoulder shaping, ending at side edge.

Shape Shoulder

Cast off 14 (17: 20: 23: 26) sts at beg of next row. Work 1 row.
Cast off rem 14 (18: 20: 23: 26) sts.
With right side facing, slip center 28 (28: 30: 30: 30) sts onto a holder, rejoin yarn to rem sts and k to end.
Complete as given for first side.

SLEEVES

With 2 ¾mm (No 12/US 2) needles, cast on 54 (54: 58: 62: 66) sts.
1st rib row (right side) K2, [p2, k2] to end.
2nd row P2, [k2, p2] to end.
Rep last 2 rows until cuff measures 5cm/2in, ending with a wrong side row and inc 4 (8: 8: 8: 8) sts evenly across last row. 58 (62: 66: 70: 74) sts.
Change to 3 ¼mm (No 10/US 3) needles.
Beg with a k row, work in st st inc one st at each end of 3rd row and every foll 4th row until there are 84 (96: 104: 112: 124) sts.
Cont straight until Sleeve measures 23 (27: 30: 35: 40)cm/9 (10 ½: 11 ¾: 13 ¾: 15 ¾)in from beg, ending with a p row.
Cast off.

COLLAR

Join shoulder seams.
With right side facing, slip first 14 (14: 15: 15: 15) sts from center front holder onto spare needle, using set of four 2 ¾mm (No 12/US 2) double pointed needles, k rem 14 (14: 15: 15: 15) sts, k up 20 (22: 22: 24: 26) sts up right front neck, k back neck sts, k up 20 (22: 22: 24: 26) sts down left front neck, then k sts from spare needle. 110 (116: 120: 126: 132) sts.
Work 10 (10: 12: 14: 14) rounds of k1, p1 rib.
Work forwards and backwards as follows:
Next row K80 (84: 87: 91: 95), turn.
Next row K50 (52: 54: 56: 58), turn.
Next row K54 (56: 58: 60: 62), turn.
Next row K58 (60: 62: 64: 66), turn.
Cont in this way, working 4 sts more at end of foll 6 rows.
Next row K to end.
Cont in garter st (every row k) for a further 4 (5: 5: 6: 6)cm/1 ½ (2: 2: 2 ½: 2 ½)in.
Cast off loosely.

TO MAKE UP

Sew on sleeves, placing center of sleeves to shoulder seams. Beg at top of side edge borders, join side and sleeve seams.

Right: Lace-edged Cardigan (see page 43) and Floral Cardigan (see page 47).

Lace-edged Cardigan

MATERIALS
9 (10: 11) 50g balls of Rowan Cotton Glace.
Pair each of 3mm (No 11/US 2) and 3 ¾mm (No 9/US 4) knitting needles.
Cable needle.
4 (4: 5) buttons.

TENSION
24 sts and 30 rows to 10cm/4in square over double moss stitch on 3 ¾mm (No 9/US 4) needles.

ABBREVIATIONS
C2B = sl next st onto cable needle and leave at back of work, k1, then k1 from cable needle;
C2F = sl next st onto cable needle and leave at front of work, k1, then k1 from cable needle;
C4B = sl next 2 sts onto cable needle and leave at back of work, k2, then k2 from cable needle;
C4F = sl next 2 sts onto cable needle and leave at front of work, k2, then k2 from cable needle;
Cr2L = sl next st onto cable needle and leave at front of work, p1, then k1 from cable needle;
Cr2R = sl next st onto cable needle and leave at back of work, k1, then p1 from cable needle;
Cr3L = sl next 2 sts onto cable needle and leave at front of work, p1, then k2 from cable needle;
Cr3R = sl next st onto cable needle and leave at back of work, k2, then p1 from cable needle;
mb = [k1, p1, k1, p1] all in next st, turn, p4, turn, k4, then pass 2nd, 3rd and 4th st over 1st st.
Also see page 8.

PANEL A
Worked over 9 sts.
1st row (right side) P1, Cr3L, p5.
2nd row K5, p2, k2.
3rd row P1, k1, Cr3L, p4.
4th row K4, p2, k1, p1, k1.
5th row P2, k1, Cr3L, p3.
6th row K3, p2, k1, p1, k2.
7th row [P1, k1] twice, Cr3L, p2.
8th row K2, p2, k1, [p1, k1] twice.
9th row P2, k1, p1, k1, Cr3L, p1.
10th row K1, p2, [k1, p1] twice, k2.

MEASUREMENTS

To fit age	4-6	6–8	8-10	years
Actual chest measurement	86 / 33 ¾	94 / 36 ¾	103 / 40 ¾	cm / in
Length	35 / 13 ¾	38 / 15	43 / 17	cm / in
Sleeve seam	30 / 12	32 / 12 ¾	38 / 15	cm / in

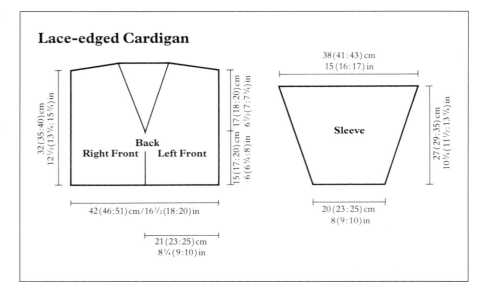

Lace-edged Cardigan

11th row P1, [k1, p1] twice, Cr3R, p1.
12th row As 8th row.
13th row P2, k1, p1, Cr3R, p2.
14th row As 6th row.
15th row P1, k1, p1, Cr3R, p3.
16th row As 4th row.
17th row P2, Cr3R, p4.
18th row As 2nd row.
19th row P1, Cr3R, p5.
20th row K6, p2, k1.
These 20 rows form patt.

PANEL B
Worked over 16 sts.
1st row (right side) *P6, C2B**, C2F, p6***.
2nd row *K5, Cr2L, p1**, p1, Cr2R, k5***.
3rd row *P4, Cr2R, C2B**, C2F, Cr2L, p4***.
4th row *K3, Cr2L, k1, p2**, p2, k1, Cr2R, k3***.
5th row *P2, Cr2R, p1, Cr2R, k1**, k1, Cr2L, p1, Cr2L, p2***.
6th row *[K2, p1] twice, k1, p1**, p1, k1, [p1, k2] twice***.
7th row *P2, mb, p1, Cr2R, p1, k1**, k1, p1, Cr2L, p1, mb, p2***.
8th row *K4, p1, k2, p1**, p1, k2, p1, k4***.
9th row *P4, mb, p2, k1**, k1, p2, mb, p4***.
10th row *K7, p1**, p1, k7***.
These 10 rows form patt.

PANEL C
Worked over 9 sts.
1st row (right side) P5, Cr3R, p1.
2nd row K2, p2, k5.
3rd row P4, Cr3R, k1, p1.
4th row K1, p1, k1, p2, k4.
5th row P3, Cr3R, k1, p2.
6th row K2, p1, k1, p2, k3.
7th row P2, Cr3R, [k1, p1] twice.
8th row K1, [p1, k1] twice, p2, k2.
9th row P1, Cr3R, k1, p1, k1, p2.
10th row K2, [p1, k1] twice, p2, k1.
11th row P1, Cr3L, [p1, k1] twice, p1.
12th row As 8th row.
13th row P2, Cr3L, p1, k1, p2.
14th row As 6th row.
15th row P3, Cr3L, p1, k1, p1.
16th row As 4th row.
17th row P4, Cr3L, p2.
18th row As 2nd row.
19th row P5, Cr3L, p1.
20th row K1, p2, k6.
These 20 rows form patt.

BACK
With 3 ¾mm (No 9/US 4) needles, cast on 120 (128: 140) sts.
1st row (right side) [K1, p1] 1 (3: 6) times, [k4, work 1st row of panel A, k4, work 1st row of panel B from * to ***] twice, k4, work 1st row of panel C, k4, work 1st row of panel B from * to ***, k4, work 1st row of panel C, k4, [p1, k1] 1 (3: 6) times.
2nd row [P1, k1] 1 (3: 6) times, [p4, work 2nd row of panel C, p4, work 2nd row of panel B from * to ***] twice, p4, work 2nd row of panel A, p4, work 2nd row of panel B from * to ***, p4, work 2nd row of panel A, p4, [k1, p1] 1 (3: 6) times.
3rd row [P1, k1] 1 (3: 6) times, [C4F, work 3rd row of panel A, C4B, work 3rd row of panel B from * to ***] twice, C4F, work 3rd row of panel C, C4B, work 3rd row of panel B from * to ***, C4F, work 3rd row of panel C, C4B, [k1, p1] 1 (3: 6) times.
4th row [K1, p1] 1 (3: 6) times, [p4, work 4th row of panel C, p4, work 4th row of panel B from * to ***] twice, p4, work 4th row of panel A, p4, work 4th row of panel B from * to ***, p4, work 4th row of panel A,

p4, [p1, k1] 1 (3: 6) times.
These 4 rows set position of panels and form cable patt between panels and double moss st at side edges. Cont in patt until Back measures 32 (35: 40)cm/12 ½ (13 ¾: 15 ¾)in from beg, ending with a wrong side row.

Shape Shoulders
Cast off 20 (21: 24) sts at beg of next 2 rows and 20 (22: 24) sts at beg of foll 2 rows. Cast off rem 40 (42: 44) sts, working [k2 tog] twice over each cable and at center of panel B and k2 tog at center of panel A and C.

LEFT FRONT
With 3 ¾mm (No 9/US 4) needles, cast on 61 (65: 71) sts.
1st row (right side) [K1, p1] 1 (3: 6) times, k4, work 1st row of panel A, k4, work 1st row of panel B from * to ***, k4, work 1st row of panel A, k4, work 1st row of panel B from * to ***, k1.
2nd row P1, work 2nd row of panel B from ** to ***, p4, work 2nd row of panel A, p4, work 2nd row of panel B from * to ***, p4, work 2nd row of panel A, p4, [k1, p1] 1 (3: 6) times.
3rd row [P1, k1] 1 (3: 6) times, C4F, work 3rd row of panel A, C4B, work 3rd row of panel B from * to ***, C4F, work 3rd row of panel A, C4B, work 3rd row of panel B from * to **, k1.
4th row P1, work 4th row of panel B from ** to ***, p4, work 4th row of panel A, p4, work 4th row of panel B from * to ***, p4, work 4th row of panel A, p4, [p1, k1] 1 (3: 6) times.
These 4 rows set position of panels and form cable patt between panels and double moss st at side edges. Cont in patt until Front measures 15 (17: 20)cm/6 (6 ¾: 8)in from beg, ending with a wrong side row.

Shape Neck

Keeping patt correct, dec one st at front edge on next row and every foll alt row until 40 (43: 48) sts rem. Cont straight until Front matches Back to shoulder shaping, ending at side edge.

Shape Shoulder

Cast off 20 (21: 24) sts at beg of next row. Work 1 row. Cast off rem 20 (22: 24) sts.

RIGHT FRONT

With 3 ¾mm (No 9/US 4) needles cast on 61 (65: 71) sts.

1st row (right side) K1, work 1st row of panel B from ** to ***, k4, work first row of panel C, k4, work 1st row of panel B from * to ***, k4, work 1st row of panel C, k4, [p1, k1] 1 (3: 6) times.

2nd row [P1, k1] 1 (3: 6) times, p4, work 2nd row of panel C, p4, work 2nd row of panel B from * to ***, p4, work 2nd row of panel C, p4, work 2nd row of panel B from * to **, p1.

3rd row K1, work 3rd row of panel B from ** to ***, C4F, work 3rd row of panel C, C4B, work 3rd row of panel B from * to ***, C4F, work 3rd row of panel C, C4B, [k1, p1] 1 (3: 6) times.

4th row [K1, p1] 1 (3: 6) times, p4, work 4th row of panel C, p4, work 4th row of panel B from * to ***, p4, work 4th row of panel C, p4, work 4th row of panel B from * to **, p1.

These 4 rows set position of panels and form cable patt between panels and double moss st at side edge. Complete as given for Left Front.

SLEEVES

With 3 ¾mm (No 9/US 4) needles cast on 58 (66: 70) sts.

1st row (right side) [K1, p1] 2 (4: 5) times, k4, work 1st row of panel A, k4, work 1st row of panel B from * to ***, k4, work 1st row of panel C, k4, [p1, k1] 2 (4: 5) times.

2nd row [P1, k1] 2 (4: 5) times, p4, work 2nd row of panel C, p4, work 2nd row of panel B from * to ***, p4, work 2nd row of panel A, p4, [k1, p1] 2 (4: 5) times.

3rd row [P1, k1] 2 (4: 5) times, C4B, work 3rd row of panel A, C4F, work 3rd row of panel B from * to ***, C4B, work 3rd row of panel C, C4F, [k1, p1] 2 (4: 5) times.

4th row [K1, p1] 2 (4: 5) times, p4, work 4th row of panel C, p4, work 4th row of panel B from * to ***, p4, work 4th row of panel A, p4, [p1, k1] 2 (4: 5) times.

These 4 rows set position of panels and form cable patt between panels and double moss st at side edges. Cont in patt, inc one st at each end of next row and every foll 3rd (3rd: 4th) row until there are 100 (108: 112) sts, working inc stitches into double moss st.

Cont straight until Sleeve measures 27 (29: 35)cm/10 ¾ (11 ½: 13 ¾)in from beg, ending with a wrong side row.
Cast off.

BUTTON BAND

With 3mm (No 11/US 2) needles cast on 8 sts.

Work in p1, k1 rib until band, when slightly stretched, fits along straight front edge of Left Front. Cast off in rib. Sew band in place.

Mark band to indicate positions of 4 (4: 5) buttons: first one 2cm/ ½in up from lower edge, last one 1 cm/ ¼in below top edge and rem 2 (2: 3) evenly spaced between.

BUTTONHOLE BAND

With 3mm (No 11/US 2) needles cast on 8 sts. Work in k1, p1 rib until first marker on Button Band is reached.

Buttonhole row (right side) Rib 2, k2 tog, yf, rib to end.

Complete as given for Button Band, making buttonholes at markers as before.

WELT EDGING

With 3mm (No 11/US 2) needles cast on 4 sts.

K 1 row.

1st row K2, yf, k2.

2nd row and 2 foll alt rows (right side) Sl1, k to end.

3rd row K3, yf, k2.

5th row K2, yf, k2 tog, yf, k2.

7th row K3, yf, k2 tog, yf, k2.

8th row Cast off 4, k to end.

These 8 rows form patt. Cont in patt until edging, when slightly stretched, fits along lower edges of Fronts and Back, ending with 8th row of patt.
Cast off.

SLEEVE EDGINGS (make 2)

Work as given for Welt Edging until edging fits along lower edge of sleeve, ending with 8th row of patt.
Cast off.

COLLAR

Join shoulder seams.

Work as given for Welt Edging, inc one st at beg of 3rd row of patt and 12 foll 4th rows, working inc sts as k.

Cont straight until shaped edge of Collar, when slightly stretched, fits up shaped edge of Right Front to center of back neck, ending with 8th row of patt. Work other half of Collar to match, working dec instead of inc and ending with 8th row of patt.
Cast off.

TO MAKE UP

Sew sleeve edgings in place. Sew on sleeves, placing center of sleeves to shoulder seams. Join side and sleeve seams. Sew on welt edging and collar in place, catching cast on and off sts of collar to center of front bands. Sew on buttons.

Floral Cardigan

MATERIALS
7 (8: 9) 50g balls of Rowan Cotton Glace in Cream (A).
1 ball of same in each of Dark Green, Purple, Brown, Lilac and Light Green.
Pair each of 3 ¼mm (No 10/US 3) and 3 ¾mm (No 9/US 4) knitting needles.
6 buttons.

TENSION
23 sts and 32 rows to 10cm/4in square over st st on 3 ¾mm (No 9/US 4) needles.

ABBREVIATIONS
See page 8.

NOTES
Read charts from right to left on right side (k) rows and from left to right on wrong side (p) rows. When working flower motifs, use separate lengths of contrast colors on each colored area and twist yarns together on wrong side at joins to avoid holes.

BACK
With 3 ¼mm (No 10/US 3) needles and A, cast on 93 (103: 111) sts.
1st row K1, [p1, k1] to end.
This row forms moss st. Moss st 7 rows more.
Change to 3 ¾mm (No 9/US 4) needles.
Beg with a k row, work 6 rows in st st.
Next row (right side) K11 (15: 17)A, k 1st row of chart 1, k33 (35: 39)A, k 1st row of chart 1, with A, k to end.
Next row P11 (15: 17)A, p 2nd row of chart 1, p33 (35: 39)A, p 2nd row of chart 1, with A, p to end.
Work a further 11 rows as set. With A and beg with a p row, work 19 rows in st st.
1st row K19 (24: 28)A, k 1st row of chart 2, k21A, k 1st row of chart 2, with A, k to end.
2nd row P19 (24: 28)A, p 2nd row of chart 2, p21A, p 2nd row of chart 2, with A, p to end.
Work a further 7 rows as set.
With A, work 12 rows.

MEASUREMENTS

To fit age	4-6	6–8	8-10	years
Actual chest measurement	80 / 31 ½	89 / 35	96 / 38	cm / in
Length	35 / 13 ¾	38 / 15	43 / 17	cm / in
Sleeve seam	32 / 12 ½	35 / 13 ½	38 / 15	cm / in

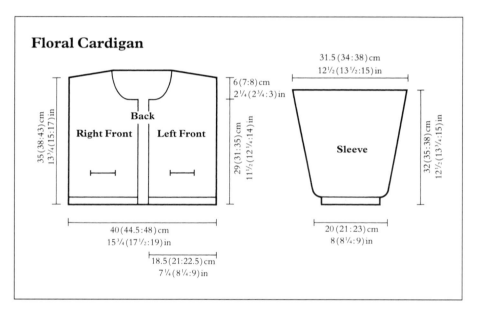

22nd row P6 (10: 12)A, p 1st row of chart 2, [p15 (16: 18)A, p 1st row of chart 2] twice, with A, p to end.

23rd row K6 (10: 12)A, k 2nd row of chart 2, [k15 (16: 18)A, k 2nd row of chart 2] twice, with A, k to end.

Work a further 7 rows as set.

With A work 12 rows.

The last 42 rows form patt. Cont in patt until Back measures 35 (38: 43)cm/13 ¾ (15: 17)in from beg, ending with a wrong side row.

Shape Shoulders

Cast off 14 (15: 17) sts at beg of next 2 rows and 14 (16: 17) sts at beg of foll 2 rows.

Leave rem 37 (41: 43) sts on a holder.

POCKET LININGS (make 2)

With 3 ¾mm (No 9/US 4) needles and A, cast on 27 sts.

Beg with a k row, work 26 rows in st st.

Leave these sts on a holder.

LEFT FRONT

With 3 ¼mm (No 10/US 3) needles and A, cast on 43 (47: 51) sts.

Work 8 rows in moss st as given for Back, inc one st at center of last row on 2nd and 3rd sizes only. 43 (48: 52) sts.

Change to 3 ¾mm (No 9/US 4) needles.

Beg with a k row, work 6 rows in st st.

Next row (right side) K11 (15: 17)A, k 1st row of chart 1, with A, k to end.

Next row P13 (14: 16)A, p 2nd row of chart 1, with A, p to end.

Work a further 11 rows as set.

Cont in A only. Beg with a p row, work 5 rows in st st.

Next row K8 (12: 14), p1, [k1, p1] 12 times, k to end.

Next row P9 (10: 12), k1, [p1, k1] 13 times, p to end.

Rep last 2 rows once more, then work 1st of the 2 rows again.

Next row P9 (10: 12), cast off in moss st next 27 sts, p to end.

Place Pocket

Next row K7 (11: 13), k across sts of pocket lining, k to end.

Work a further 7 rows in st st.

1st row K19 (24: 28)A, k 1st row of chart 2, k7A.

2nd row P7A, p 2nd row of chart 2, with A, p to end.

Work a further 7 rows as set.

With A, work 12 rows.

22nd row P20 (21: 23)A, p 1st row of chart 2, with A p to end.

23rd row K6 (10: 12)A, k 2nd row of chart 2, with A, k to end.

Work a further 7 rows as set.

With A, work 12 rows.

The last 42 rows form patt. Cont in patt until Front measures 29 (31: 35)cm/11 ½ (12 ¼: 14)in from beg, ending with a right side row.

Shape Neck

Keeping patt correct, cast off 4 sts at beg of next row and foll alt row. Dec one st at neck edge on next 5 rows, then on every alt row until 28 (31: 34) sts rem. Cont straight until Front matches Back to shoulder shaping, ending with a wrong side row.

Shape Shoulder

Cast off 14 (15: 17) sts at beg of next row.

Work 1 row.

Cast off rem 14 (16: 17) sts.

RIGHT FRONT

With 3 ¼mm (No 10/US 3) needles and A, cast on 43 (47: 51) sts.

Work 8 rows in moss st as given for Back, inc one st at center of last row on 2nd and 3rd sizes only. 43 (48: 52) sts.

Change to 3 ¾mm (No 9/US 4) needles.

Beg with a k row, work 6 rows in st st.

Next row (right side) K13 (14: 16)A, k 1st row of chart 1, with A, k to end.

Next row P11 (15: 17)A, p 2nd row of chart 1, with A, p to end.

Work a further 11 rows as set.

Cont in A only. Beg with a p row, work 5 rows in st st.

Next row K10 (11: 13), p1, [k1, p1] 12 times, k to end.

Next row P7 (11: 13), k1, [p1, k1] 13 times, p to end.

Rep last 2 rows once more, then work 1st of the 2 rows again.

Next row P7 (11: 13), cast off in moss st next 27 sts, p to end.

Place Pocket

Next row K9 (10: 12), k across sts of pocket lining, k to end.

Work a further 7 rows in st st.

1st row K7A, k 1st row of chart 2, with A, k to end.

2nd row P19 (24: 28)A, p 2nd row of chart 2, p7A.

Work a further 7 rows as set.

With A, work 12 rows.

22nd row P6 (10: 12)A, p 1st row of chart 2, with A, p to end.

23rd row K20 (21: 23)A, k 2nd row of chart 2, with A, k to end.

Work a further 7 rows as set.

With A, work 12 rows.

The last 42 rows form patt.

Complete to match Left Front, reversing shapings.

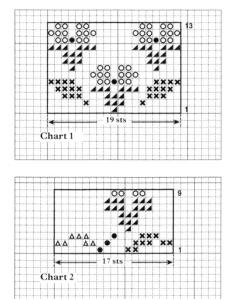

Chart 1 — 19 sts — 13, 1

Chart 2 — 17 sts — 9, 1

KEY

- ☐ Cream (A)
- ☒ Dark Green
- ◪ Purple
- ◉ Brown
- ⊙ Lilac
- ◿ Light Green

SLEEVES

With 3 ¼mm (No 10/US 3) needles and A, cast on 43 (45: 47) sts.
Work 8 rows in moss st as given for Back, inc 4 sts evenly across last row. 47 (49: 51) sts.
Change to 3 ¾mm (No 9/US 4) needles. Beg with a k row, work 6 rows in st st, inc one st at each end of 5th row. 49 (51: 53) sts.
Next row (right side) K15 (16: 17)A, k 1st row of chart 1, with A, k to end.
Next row P15 (16: 17)A, p 2nd row of chart 1, with A, p to end.
Work a further 11 rows as set, inc one st at each end of 3rd row and foll 6th row.
With A, work 19 rows in st st, inc one st at each end of 4th row and 2 foll 6th rows. 59 (61: 63) sts.
Next row K2 (3: 4)A, k 1st row of chart 2, k21A, k 1st row of chart 2, with A, k to end.
Next row P2 (3: 4)A, p 2nd row of chart 2, p21A, p 2nd row of chart 2, with A, p to end.
Work a further 7 rows as set, inc one st at each end of 1st row and foll 6th row.
With A, work 12 rows, inc one st at each end of 2 foll 6th rows, 67 (69: 71) sts.
Next row P25 (26: 27)A, p 1st row of chart 2, with A, p to end.
Next row K25 (26: 27)A, k 2nd row of chart 2, with A, k to end.
Work a further 7 rows as set, inc one st at each end of 4th row.
With A, work 12 rows, inc one st at each end of 3rd row and foll 6th row. 73 (75: 77) sts.
The last 42 rows set patt.

2nd and 3rd sizes only

Cont in patt, inc one st at each end of 2nd row and (1: 2) foll 6th rows. (79: 83) sts.

All sizes

Cont straight in patt until Sleeve measures 32 (35: 38)cm/12 ½ (13 ¾: 15)in from beg, ending with a wrong side row.
Cast off.

NECKBAND

Join shoulder seams.
With 3 ¼mm (No 10/US 3) needles, A and right side facing, k up 23 (26: 29) sts up right front neck, k back neck sts dec 4 sts evenly, k up 23 (26: 29) sts down left front neck. 79 (89: 97) sts.
Moss st 8 rows.
Cast off in moss st.

BUTTON BAND

With 3 ¼mm (No 10/US 3) needles and A, cast on 8 sts.
1st row [K1, p1] to end.
2nd row [P1, k1] to end.
These 2 rows form moss st. Cont in moss st until band, when slightly stretched, fits up Left Front to top of neckband. Cast off.
Sew band in position. Mark band to indicate position of 6 buttons: first one 4 rows up from lower edge, last one 4 rows down from top edge and rem evenly spaced between.

BUTTONHOLE BAND

Work as given for Button Band, but beg moss st with 2nd row and making buttonholes to match markers as follows:
Buttonhole row Moss st 2, p2 tog, yrn, moss st 4.

TO MAKE UP

Sew on sleeves, placing center of sleeves to shoulder seams. Join side and sleeve seams. Catch down pocket linings. Sew on buttons.

Moss-stitch Tunic with Hat

MATERIALS
Tunic 4 (5: 6: 8: 9: 10) 50g hanks of Rowan DK Tweed.
Pair each of 3 ¼mm (No 10/US 3) and 4mm (No 8/US 6) knitting needles.
3 (3: 3: 4: 4: 4) buttons.
Hat 1 (2) 50g hank of Rowan DK Tweed.
Pair each of 4mm (No 8/US 6) knitting needles.

TENSION
21 sts and 36 rows to 10cm/4in square in moss st on 4mm (No 8/US 6) needles.

ABBREVIATIONS
See page 8.

TUNIC
BACK
With 4mm (No 8/US 6) needles cast on 67 (73: 85: 95: 105: 115) sts.
1st row K1, [p1, k1] to end.
This row forms moss st. Cont in moss st until Back measures 33 (38: 45: 50: 55: 60)cm/13 (15: 17 ¾: 19 ¾: 21 ¾: 23 ¾)in from beg.

Shape Shoulders
Cast off 10 (11: 14: 16: 18: 20) sts at beg of next 4 rows. Leave rem 27 (29: 29: 31: 33: 35) sts on a holder.

FRONT
Work as given for Back until Front measures 21 (22: 29: 32: 35: 40)cm/8 ¼ (8 ¾: 11 ½: 12 ½: 13 ¾: 15 ¾)in from beg.

Divide for Opening
Next row Patt 31 (34: 40: 45: 50: 55), turn; leave rem 36 (39: 45: 50: 55: 60) sts on a spare needle.
Cast on 5 sts at beg of next row for button band.
Cont in patt on this set of 36 (39: 45: 50: 55: 60) sts until Front measures 28 (33: 40: 44: 49: 54)cm/11 (13: 15 ¾: 17 ¼: 19 ¼: 21 ¼)in from beg, ending at inside edge.

MEASUREMENTS

TUNIC

To fit age	1	1-2	3-4	4-6	6–8	8-10	years
Actual chest	64	69	80	90	100	109	cm
measurement	25	27	31 ½	35 ½	39 ½	43	in
Length	33	38	45	50	55	60	cm
	13	15	17 ¾	19 ¾	21 ¾	23 ¾	in
Sleeve seam	20	23	28	32	38	40	cm
(with cuff	8	9	11	12 ½	15	15 ¾	in
turned back)							

HAT

To fit age	1-2	2-6	years

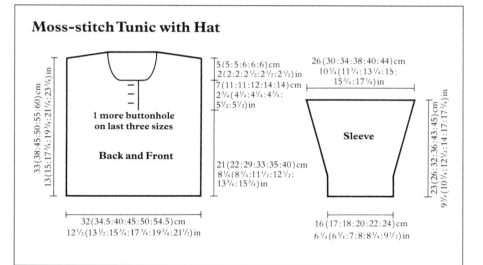

Moss-stitch Tunic with Hat

33(38:45:50:55:60) cm
13(15:17¾:19¾:21¼:23¾)in

1 more buttonhole
on last three sizes

Back and Front

5(5:5:6:6:6)cm
2(2:2:2½:2½:2½)in
7(11:11:12:14:14)cm
2¾(4¼:4¼:4¾:5½:5½)in

21(22:29:33:35:40)cm
8¼(8¾:11½:12½:13¾:15¾)in

32(34.5:40:45:50:54.5)cm
12½(13½:15¾:17¾:19¾:21½)in

26(30:34:38:40:44)cm
10¼(11¾:13¼:15:15¾:17¼)in

Sleeve

23(26:32:36:43:45)cm
9¼(10¼:12½:14:17:17¾)in

16(17:18:20:22:24)cm
6¼(6¾:7:8:8¾:9½)in

Shape Neck

Next row Cast off 3, patt 4 sts more, leave these 5 sts on a safety pin, patt to end.
Dec one st at neck edge on next 5 (7: 7: 7: 9: 9) rows, then on every foll alt row until 20 (22: 28: 32: 36: 40) sts rem.
Cont straight until Front matches Back to shoulder shaping, ending at side edge.

Shape Shoulder

Cast off 10 (11: 14: 16: 18: 20) sts at beg of next row. Work 1 row.
Cast off rem 10 (11: 14: 16: 18: 20) sts.
Mark button band to indicate position of 3 (3: 3: 4: 4: 4) buttons: first one 2 (3: 3: 2: 4: 4)cm/ ¾ (1 ¼: 1 ¼: ¾: 1 ½: 1 ½)in from cast on edge, last one 1cm/ ¼in below neck shaping and rem 1 (1: 1: 2: 2: 2) evenly spaced between.
Rejoin yarn at inside edge to sts on a spare needle and patt to end. Patt a further 2 (3: 3: 2: 4: 4)cm/ ¾ (1 ¼: 1 ¼: ¾: 1 ½: 1 ½)in, ending at inside edge.
Buttonhole row Patt 2, p2 tog, yrn, patt to end.
Complete as given for first side, making buttonholes at markers as before.

SLEEVES

With 4mm (No 8/US 6) needles cast on 33 (35: 39: 43: 47: 51) sts.
Work 3 (3: 4: 4: 5: 5)cm/1 ¼ (1 ¼: 1 ½: 1 ½: 2: 2)in in moss st as given for Back.
Change to 3 ¼mm (No 10/US 6) needles.
Cont in moss st for a further 3 (3: 4: 4: 5: 5)cm/1 ¼ (1 ¼: 1 ½: 1 ½: 2: 2)in.
Change to 4mm (No 8/US 6) needles.
Cont in moss st, inc one st at each end of next row and every foll 4th (4th: 4th: 5th: 5th: 5th) row until there are 55 (63: 71: 79: 85: 93) sts, working inc sts into patt.
Cont straight until Sleeve measures 23 (26: 32: 36: 43: 45)cm/9 ¼ (10 ¼: 12 ½: 14: 17: 17 ¾)in from beg.
Cast off.

COLLAR

Join shoulder seams.
With 3 ¼mm (No 10/US 3) needles and right side facing, sl 5 sts on right side front safety pin onto needle, k up 11 (12: 12: 15: 16: 17) sts up right front neck, moss st across back neck sts, k up 11 (12: 12: 15: 16: 17) sts down left front neck, moss st 5 sts from left side front safety pin. 59 (63: 63: 71: 75: 79) sts. Moss st 1 row across all sts.
Next 2 rows Moss st to last 17 (17: 17: 21: 21: 21) sts, turn.
Next 2 rows Moss st to last 14 (14: 14: 17: 17: 17) sts, turn.
Next 2 rows Moss st to last 11 (11: 11: 13: 13: 13) sts, turn.
Next 2 rows Moss st to last 8 (8: 8: 9: 9: 9) sts, turn.
Cont in moss st across all sts, inc one st at each end of 5 foll 4th rows.
Moss st 2 rows.
Cast off in moss st.

TO MAKE UP

Sew on sleeves, placing center of sleeves to shoulder seams. Join side and sleeve seams. Catch down cast on edge of button band on wrong side.
Sew on buttons.

HAT

EAR FLAPS (make 2)

With 4mm (No 8/US 6) needles cast on 9 sts.
1st row K1, [p1, k1] to end.
This row forms moss st. Cont in moss st, inc one st at each end of next row and 3 (4) foll alt rows. 17 (19) sts.
Moss st 6 (10) rows straight.
Dec one st at each end of next row and foll alt row.
Now inc one st at each end of 2nd row and 2 foll rows. 19 (21) sts.
Moss st 1 row. Leave these sts on a holder.

MAIN PART

With 4mm (No 8/US 6) needles cast on 11 (13) sts, moss st across first ear flap, cast on 33 (37) sts, moss st across second ear flap, cast on 12 (14) sts. 94 (104) sts.
Cont in moss st, work 29 (33) rows.

Shape Top

1st row [Moss st 15 (17), work 3 tog] 5 times, moss st 4.
Moss st 3 rows.
5th row [Moss st 13 (15), work 3 tog] 5 times, moss st 4.
Moss st 3 rows.
9th row [Moss st 11 (13), work 3 tog] 5 times, moss st 4.
Cont in this way, dec 10 sts as set on every foll 4th row until 34 sts rem. Work 1 row.
Next row [Moss st 7, work 3 tog, moss st 7] twice.
Work 1 row.
Next row [Moss st 6, work 3 tog, moss st 6] twice.
Work 1 row.
Next row [Moss st 5, work 3 tog, moss st 5] twice.
Cont in this way, dec 4 sts as set on every foll alt row until 6 sts rem.
Work 1 row.
Break off yarn, thread end through rem sts, pull up and secure.
Join back seam.

Guernsey with Ribbed Yoke

MATERIALS
3 (4: 5: 5: 6: 7) 50g balls of Rowan True
4 ply Botany.
Pair each of 3mm (No 11/US 2) and
3 ¼mm (No 10/US 3) knitting needles.
3 buttons for 1st and 2nd sizes only.

TENSION
28 sts and 36 rows to 10cm/4in square over
st st on 3 ¼mm (No 10/US 3) needles.

ABBREVIATIONS
See page 8.

BACK
With 3mm (No 11/US 2) needles cast on 88
(98: 113: 128: 143: 158) sts.
K 9 (9: 11: 11: 13: 13) rows.
Change to 3 ¼mm (No 10/US 3) needles.
Beg with a k row, work in st st until Back
measures 18 (21: 25: 28: 31: 34)cm/7 (8 ¼:
10: 11: 12 ¼: 13 ¼)in from beg, ending
with a p row.
Next row (right side) K3, [p2, k3] to end.
Next row P.
The last 2 rows form yoke patt. Cont in
yoke patt until Back measures 31 (36: 43:
48: 53: 58)cm/12 ¼ (14 ¼: 17: 18 ¾: 20 ¾:
22 ¾)in from beg, ending with a wrong side
row.

Shape Neck
Next row Patt 31 (35: 40: 48: 53: 59), turn.
Work on this set of sts only. Keeping patt
correct, dec one st at neck edge on next 6
(6: 6: 8: 8: 8) rows. Patt 1 row.
Cast off rem 25 (29: 34: 40: 45: 51) sts.
With right side facing, slip center 26 (28:
33: 32: 37: 40) sts onto a holder, rejoin yarn
to rem sts, patt to end.
Complete as given for first side.

FRONT
Work as given for Back, until Front
measures 29 (34: 40: 45: 49: 54)cm/11 ½
(13 ½: 15 ¾: 17 ½: 19 ¼: 21 ¼)in from
beg, ending with a wrong side row.

Shape Neck
Next row Patt 35 (39: 45: 51: 57: 64), turn.
Work on this set of sts only. Dec one st at
neck edge on every row until 25 (29: 34: 40:
45: 51) sts rem.
Cont straight until Front matches Back to

cast off edge, ending with a wrong side row.
Cast off.
With right side facing, slip center 18 (20:
23: 26: 29: 30) sts onto a holder, rejoin yarn
to rem sts, patt to end.
Complete as given for first side.

SLEEVES
With 3mm (No 11/US 2) needles cast on
50 (54: 54: 58: 58: 62) sts.
1st rib row (right side) K2, [p2, k2] to end.
2nd rib row P2, [k2, p2] to end.
Rib a further 8 (10: 12: 14: 16: 18) rows, inc
2 (4: 5: 5: 7: 6) sts evenly across last row. 52

(58: 59: 63: 65: 68) sts.
Change to 3 ¼mm (No 10/US 3) needles.
Beg with a k row, work in st st, inc one st at
each end of 5th row and every foll 4th row
until there are 68 (78: 83: 93: 103: 108) sts,
ending with a p row.
Now work in yoke patt as given for Back,
inc one st at each end of 4th row and every
foll 6th (4th: 4th: 4th: 4th: 4th) row until
there are 72 (84: 95: 105: 115: 122) sts,
working inc sts into patt.
Cont straight until Sleeve measures 20 (23:
28: 32: 38: 40)cm/8 (9: 11: 12 ½: 15: 15 ¾)in
from beg, ending with a wrong side row.
Cast off.

To fit age	1	2-3	4-5	6-7	8–9	9-10	years
Actual chest measurement	62 / 24 ½	70 / 27 ½	80 / 31 ½	91 / 36	102 / 40	112 / 44	cm / in
Length	33 / 13	38 / 15	45 / 17 ¾	51 / 20	56 / 22	61 / 24	cm / in
Sleeve seam	20 / 8	23 / 9	28 / 11	32 / 12 ½	38 / 15	40 / 15 ¾	cm / in

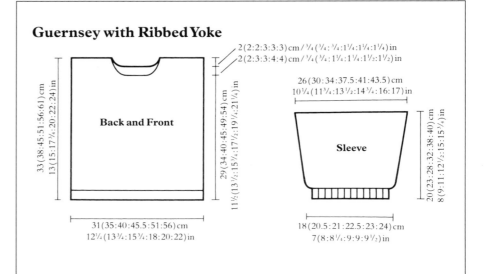

Guernsey with Ribbed Yoke

NECKBAND

Join right shoulder seam.

With 3mm (No 11/US 2) needles and right side facing, k up 15 (15: 17: 18: 20: 20) sts down left front neck, k center front sts, k up 15 (15: 17: 18: 20: 20) sts up right front neck, 8 (8: 8: 10: 10: 10) sts down right back neck, k center back sts, k up 8 (8: 8: 10: 10: 10) sts up left back neck. 90 (94: 106: 114: 126: 130) sts. Beg with a 2nd row, work 7 (9: 11: 13: 13: 15) rows in rib as given for Sleeves. Beg with a k row, work 6 (6: 8: 8: 10: 10) rows in st st.
Cast off loosely.

TO MAKE UP

1st and 2nd sizes only

With 3mm (No 11/US 2) needles and right side facing, k up 31 (36) sts along rib part of neckband and left back shoulder for button band.

K 3 rows. Cast off.

With 3mm (No 11/US 2) needles and right side facing, k up 31 (36) sts along left front shoulder and rib part of neckband for buttonhole band.

K 1 row.

Buttonhole row K7 (9), [yf, k2 tog, k8 (9)] twice, yf, k2 tog, k2 (3).

K 1 row. Cast off.

Lap buttonhole band over button band and catch together row ends at side edge. Sew on sleeves, placing center of sleeves to shoulders. Join sleeve seams, then side seams, leaving lower edging open. Sew on buttons.

3rd, 4th, 5th and 6th sizes only

Join left shoulder seam and neckband seam, reversing seam on last 5 rows of neckband. Sew on sleeves, placing center of sleeves to shoulder seams. Join sleeve seams, then side seams, leaving lower edging open.

Right: Fair Isle Sweater with Two-color Rib (see page 75), Moss and Cable Jacket with Petal Collar (see page 71) and Cable and Garter-stitch Sweater (see page 67).

Denim Wrap

MATERIALS
18 50g balls of Rowan Denim.
Pair each of 3 ¾mm (No 9/US 4) and
4 ½mm (No 7/US 7) knitting needles.
Cable needle.

TENSION
19 sts and 28 rows to 10cm/4in square over
moss st on 4 ½mm (No 7/US 7) needles
before washing.

ABBREVIATIONS
C3B = sl next st onto cable needle and
leave at back of work, k2, then k1 from
cable needle;
C3F = sl next 2 sts onto cable needle and
leave at front of work, k1, then k2 from
cable needle;
C6F = sl next 3 sts onto cable needle and
leave at front of work, k3, then k3 from
cable needle;
Cr2L = sl next st onto cable needle and
leave at front of work, p1, then k1 from
cable needle;
Cr2R = sl next st onto cable needle and
leave at back of work, k1, then p1 from
cable needle;
Cr3L = sl next 2 sts onto cable needle and
leave at front of work, p1, then k2 from
cable needle;
Cr3R = sl next st onto cable needle and
leave at back of work, k2, then p1 from
cable needle;
Also see page 8.

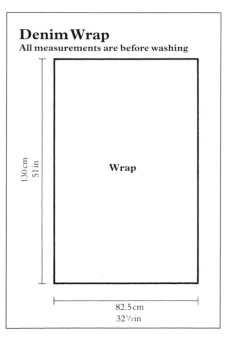

Denim Wrap
All measurements are before washing

Wrap

130cm
51in

82.5cm
32½in

PANEL A
Worked over 8 sts.
1st row (right side) K6, p1, k1.
2nd row P2, k1, p5.
3rd row K4, [p1, k1] twice.
4th row P2, k1, p1, k1, p3.
5th row K2, [p1, k1] 3 times.
6th row P2, [k1, p1] 3 times.
7th row As 5th row.
8th row As 4th row.
9th row As 3rd row.
10th row As 2nd row.
These 10 rows form patt.

PANEL B
Worked over 18 sts.
1st row (right side) P5, k8, p5.
2nd row K5, p8, k5.
3rd row P4, Cr2R, k6, Cr2L, p4.
4th row K4, p1, k1, p6, k1, p1, k4.
5th row P3, Cr2R, p1, k6, p1, Cr2L, p3.
6th row K3, p1, k2, p6, k2, p1, k3.
7th row P2, Cr2R, p2, C6F, p2, Cr2L, p2.
8th row K2, p1, k3, p6, k3, p1, k2.
9th row P1, Cr2R, p3, k6, p3, Cr2L, p1.
10th row K1, p1, k4, p6, k4, p1, k1.
11th row P1, Cr2L, p3, k6, p3, Cr2R, p1.
12th row As 8th row.
13th row P2, Cr2L, p2, C6F, p2, Cr2R, p2.
14th row As 6th row.
15th row P3, Cr2L, p1, k6, p1, Cr2R, p3.
16th row As 4th row.
17th row P4, Cr2L, k6, Cr2R, p4.
18th row K5, p8, k5.
Rows 3 to 18 form patt.

PANEL C
Worked over 8 sts.
1st row (right side) K1, p1, k6.
2nd row P5, k1, p2.
3rd row [K1, p1] twice, k4.
4th row P3, k1, p1, k1, p2.
5th row [K1, p1] 3 times, k2.
6th row [P1, k1] 3 times, p2.
7th row As 5th row.
8th row As 4th row.
9th row As 3rd row.
10th row As 2nd row.
These 10 rows form patt.

PANEL D
Worked over 14 sts.
1st row (right side) P3, k8, p3.
2nd row K3, p8, k3.
3rd row P4, C3B, Cr3L, p4.
4th row K4, p3, k1, p2, k4.
5th row P3, Cr3R, k1, p1, C3F, p3.
6th row K3, p2, [k1, p1] twice, p2, k3.
7th row P2, C3B, [p1, k1] twice, Cr3L, p2.
8th row K2, p3, [k1, p1] twice, k1, p2, k2.
9th row P1, Cr3R, [k1, p1] 3 times, C3F, p1.
10th row K1, p2, [k1, p1] 4 times, p2, k1.
11th row P1, Cr3L, [k1, p1] 3 times, Cr3R,
p1.
12th row As 8th row.
13th row P2, Cr3L, [p1, k1] twice, Cr3R, p2.
14th row As 6th row.
15th row P3, Cr3L, k1, p1, Cr3R, p3.
16th row As 4th row.
17th row P4, Cr3L, Cr3R, p4.
18th row K5, p4, k5.
19th row P3, sl next 2 sts onto cable needle
and leave at back of work, k2, then k2 from
cable needle, sl next 2 sts onto cable needle
and leave at front of work, k2, then k2 from
cable needle, p3.
20th row K3, p8, k3.
21st row P3, k8, p3.
22nd row As 20th row.
23rd and 24th rows As 19th and 20th rows.
These 24 rows form patt.

TO MAKE
With 3 ¾mm (No 9/US 4) needles cast on
171 sts.
1st row P1, [k1, p1] to end.
This row forms moss st. Moss st 4 rows more.
Inc row Moss st 17, *[inc in next st, moss
st 1] twice, [inc in next st, moss st 19]
twice; rep from * twice more, [inc in next st,
moss st 1] 3 times, moss st 16. 186 sts.
Change to 4 ½mm (No 7/US 7) needles.
1st row (right side) Moss st 4, [work 1st
row of panels A, B, C and D] 3 times, work
1st row of panels A, B and C, moss st 4.
2nd row Moss st 4, [work 2nd row of
panels C, B, A and D] 3 times, work 2nd
row of panels C, B and A, moss st 4.
These 2 rows set position of panels. Patt
375 rows more.
Dec row Patt 17, *[work 2 tog, patt 1]
twice, [work 2 tog, patt 19] twice; rep from
* twice more, [work 2 tog, patt 1] 3 times,
patt 16. 171 sts.
Change to 3 ¾mm (No 9/US 4) needles.
Work 6 rows in moss st across all sts.
Cast off in moss st.

Moss-Stitch Beret

MATERIALS
1 (2) 50g balls of Rowan Cotton Glace.
1st size Pair each of 2 ¾mm (No 12/US 1)
and 3 ¼mm (No 10/US 3) knitting needles.
2nd size Pair each of 3mm (No 11/US 2)
and 3 ¾mm (No 9/US 4) knitting needles.

ABBREVIATIONS
See page 8.

TO MAKE
With 2 ¾mm (No 12/US 1) needles for first
size, or 3mm (No 11/US 2) for second size,
cast on 96 sts.
Work 7 rows in k1, p1 rib.
Inc row Rib 3, m1, rib 3, [m1, rib 2, m1, rib
3] to end. 133 sts.
Change to 3 ¼mm (No 10/US 3) needles
for first size and 3 ¾mm (No 9/US 4)
needles for second size.
1st row K1, [p1, k1] to end.
This row forms moss st patt.
Cont in patt until work measures 9
(11)cm/3 ½ (4 ¼)in from beg.

Shape Top
Dec row [Patt 19, p3 tog,] to last st, patt 1.
Moss st 1 row.
Dec row [Patt 17, p3 tog] to last st, patt 1.
Moss st 1 row.
Dec row [Patt 15, p3 tog] to last st, patt 1.
Cont in this way, dec 12 sts as set on every
alt row until 13 sts rem.
Break off yarn, thread end through rem sts,
pull up and secure.
Join back seam.

MEASUREMENTS

To fit age	1-2	3-6	years

Left: Moss-Stitch Beret, Cable and Bobble
Tunic (see page 15), and Cream Denim Sweater
(see page 27).

Aran Sweater

MATERIALS

15 (17: 19) 50g balls of Rowan DK Handknit
Cotton.
Pair each of 3 ¼mm (No 10/US 3) and 4mm
(No 8/US 6) knitting needles.
Cable needle.

TENSION

20 sts and 28 rows to 10cm/4in square over st
st on 4mm (No 8/US 6) needles.

ABBREVIATIONS

C4B = sl next 2 sts onto cable needle and
leave at back of work, k2, then k2 from cable
needle;
C4F = sl next 2 sts onto cable needle and
leave at front of work, k2, then k2 from cable
needle;
C2BK = sl next st onto cable needle and
leave at back of work, k1 tbl, then k1 tbl from
cable needle;
C2FK = sl next st onto cable needle and
leave at front of work, k1 tbl, then k1 tbl from
cable needle;
Cr2L = sl next st onto cable needle and leave
at front of work, p1, then k1 tbl from cable
needle;
Cr2R = sl next st onto cable needle and leave
at back of work, k1 tbl, then p1 from cable
needle;
Cr3L = sl next 2 sts onto cable needle and
leave at front of work, p1, then k2 from cable
needle;
Cr3R = sl next st onto cable needle and leave
at back of work, k2, then p1 from cable
needle;
Tw2 = k into front of 2nd st on left hand
needle, then k 1st st, sl both sts of needle tog.
Also see page 8.

MEASUREMENTS

To fit age	4-7	7–9	9-10	years
Actual chest measurement	100	112	126	cm
	39 ½	44	49 ½	in
Length	52	57	62	cm
	20 ½	22 ½	24 ½	in
Sleeve seam	35	37	39	cm
	13 ¾	14 ½	15 ½	in

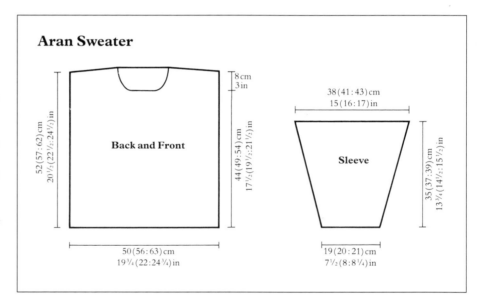

Aran Sweater

Back and Front
52(57:62)cm
20½(22½:24½)in
44(49:54)cm
17½(19½:21½)in
50(56:63)cm
19¾(22:24¾)in

Sleeve
38(41:43)cm
15(16:17)in
35(37:39)cm
13¾(14½:15½)in
19(20:21)cm
7½(8:8¼)in
8cm
3in

PANEL A

Worked over 20 sts.
1st row (right side) P6, C2BK, p1, Tw2,
p1, C2FK, p6.
2nd row K6, p2, k1, p2 tbl, k1, p2, k6.
3rd row P5, Cr2R, k1 tbl, p1, Tw2, p1, k1
tbl, Cr2L, p5.
4th row K5, [p1, k1] twice, p2 tbl, [k1, p1]
twice, k5.
5th row P4, Cr2R, C2BK, p1, Tw2, p1,
C2FK, Cr2L, p4.
6th row K4, p1, k1, p2, k1, p2 tbl, k1, p2,
k1, p1, k4.
7th row P3, [Cr2R] twice, k1 tbl, p1, Tw2,
p1, k1 tbl, [Cr2L] twice, p3.
8th row K3, [p1, k1] 3 times, p2 tbl, [k1,
p1] 3 times, k3.
9th row P2, [Cr2R] twice, C2BK, p1, Tw2,
p1, C2FK, [Cr2L] twice, p2.

10th row K2, [p1, k1] twice, p2, k1, p2 tbl,
k1, p2, [k1, p1] twice, k2.
11th row P1, [Cr2R] 3 times, k1 tbl, p1,
Tw2, p1, k1 tbl, [Cr2L] 3 times, p1.
12th row [K1, p1] 4 times, k1, p2 tbl, k1,
[p1, k1] 4 times.
13th and 14th rows As 9th and 10th rows.
15th and 16th rows As 7th and 8th rows.
17th and 18th rows As 5th and 6th rows.
19th and 20th rows As 3rd and 4th rows.
21st and 22nd rows As 1st and 2nd rows.
23rd row P7, k1 tbl, p1, Tw2, p1, k1 tbl, p7.
24th row K7, p1, k1, p2 tbl, k1, p1, k7.
25th row P9, Tw2, p9.
26th row K9, p2 tbl, k9.
27th and 28th rows As 25th and 26th rows.
These 28 rows form patt.

PANEL B

Worked over 14 sts.

1st row (right side) P4, sl next st onto cable needle and leave at back of work, k2, then k1 from cable needle, sl next 2 sts onto cable needle and leave at front of work, k1, then k2 from cable needle, p4.

2nd row K4, p6, k4.

3rd row P3, Cr3R, Tw2, Cr3L, p3.

4th row K3, [p2, k1] 3 times, k2.

5th row P2, Cr3R, p1, Tw2, p1, Cr3L, p2.

6th row [K2, p2] 3 times, k2.

7th row P1, Cr3R, p2, Tw2, p2, Cr3L, p1.

8th row K1, [p2, k3] twice, p2, k1.

9th row P1, Cr3L, p2, Tw2, p2, Cr3R, p1.

10th row As 6th row.

11th row P2, Cr3L, p1, Tw2, p1, Cr3R, p2.

12th row As 4th row.

13th row P3, Cr3L, Tw2, Cr3R, p3.

14th row As 2nd row.

15th row P4, Cr3L, Cr3R, p4.

16th row K5, p4, k5.

17th row P5, k4, p5.

18th row K5, p4, k5.

These 18 rows form patt.

PANEL C

Worked over 28 sts.

1st row (right side) [P1, k1 tbl] 7 times, [k1 tbl, p1] 7 times.

2nd row [K1, p1 tbl] 7 times, [p1 tbl, k1] 7 times.

3rd row [P1, k1 tbl] 4 times, [Cr2R] twice, C2BK, C2FK, [Cr2L] twice, [k1 tbl, p1] 4 times.

4th row [K1, p1 tbl] 4 times, [p1 tbl, k1] twice, p4 tbl, [k1, p1 tbl] twice, [p1 tbl, k1] 4 times.

5th row P1, [k1 tbl, p1] 3 times, [Cr2R] 3 times, Tw2, [Cr2L] 3 times, [p1, k1 tbl] 3 times, p1.

6th row As 2nd row.

7th row [P1, k1 tbl] 3 times, [Cr2R] 3 times, p1, Tw2, p1, [Cr2L] 3 times, [k1 tbl, p1] 3 times.

8th row [K1, p1 tbl] 3 times, [p1 tbl, k1] 3 times, k1, p2 tbl, k1, [k1, p1 tbl] 3 times, [p1 tbl, k1] 3 times.

9th row [P1, k1 tbl] twice, p1, [Cr2R] 3 times, p2, Tw2, p2, [Cr2L] 3 times, p1, [k1 tbl, p1] twice.

10th row [K1, p1 tbl] 5 times, k3, p2 tbl, k3, [p1 tbl, k1] 5 times.

11th row [P1, k1 tbl] twice, [Cr2R] 3 times, p3, Tw2, p3, [Cr2L] 3 times, [k1 tbl, p1] twice.

12th row [K1, p1 tbl] twice, [p1 tbl, k1] 3 times, k3, p2 tbl, k3, [k1, p1 tbl] 3 times, [p1 tbl, k1] twice.

13th row P1, k1 tbl, p1, [Cr2R] 3 times, p4, Tw2, p4, [Cr2L] 3 times, p1, k1 tbl, p1.

14th row [K1, p1 tbl] 4 times, k5, p2 tbl, k5, [p1 tbl, k1] 4 times.

15th row P1, k1 tbl, [Cr2R] 3 times, p5, Tw2, p5, [Cr2L] 3 times, k1 tbl, p1.

16th row K1, p2 tbl, [k1, p1 tbl] twice, k6, p2 tbl, k6, [p1 tbl, k1] twice, p2 tbl, k1.

17th row P1, k1 tbl, [Cr2L] 3 times, p5, Tw2, p5, [Cr2R] 3 times, k1 tbl, p1.

18th row As 14th row.

19th row P1, k1 tbl, p1, C2FK, [Cr2L] twice, p4, Tw2, p4, [Cr2R] twice, C2BK, p1, k1 tbl, p1.

20th row As 12th row.

21st row [P1, k1 tbl] twice, [Cr2L] 3 times, p3, Tw2, p3, [Cr2R] 3 times, [k1 tbl, p1] twice.

22nd row As 10th row.

23rd row [P1, k1 tbl] twice, p1, C2FK, [Cr2L] twice, p2, Tw2, p2, [Cr2R] twice, C2BK, p1, [k1 tbl, p1] twice.

24th row As 8th row.

25th row [P1, k1 tbl] 3 times, [Cr2L] 3 times, p1, Tw2, p1, [Cr2R] 3 times, [k1 tbl, p1] 3 times.

26th row As 2nd row.

27th row [P1, k1 tbl] 3 times, p1, C2FK, [Cr2L] twice, Tw2, [Cr2R] twice, C2BK, p1, [k1 tbl, p1] 3 times.

28th row As 4th row.

29th row [P1, k1 tbl] 4 times, [Cr2L] 3 times, [Cr2R] 3 times, [k1 tbl, p1] 4 times.

Rows 2nd to 29th form patt.

BACK

With 3 ¼mm (No 10/US 3) needles cast on 104 (120: 136) sts.

Beg with a k row, work 5 rows in st st.

Next row P5 (6: 7), *m1, p3 (4: 5), m1, p4; rep from * to last 1 (2: 3) sts, p to end. 132 (148: 164) sts.

Change to 4mm (No 8/US 6) needles.

1st row (right side) P2, [Tw2, p2] 1 (3: 5) times, k4, work 1st row of panel A, k4, work 1st row of panel B, k4, work 1st row of panel C, k4, work 1st row of panel B, k4, work 1st row of panel A, k4, [p2, Tw2] 1 (3: 5) times, p2.

2nd row K2, [p2 tbl, k2] 1 (3: 5) times, p4, work 2nd row of panel A, p4, work 2nd row of panel B, p4, work 2nd row of panel C, p4, work 2nd row of panel B, p4, work 2nd row of panel A, p4, [k2, p2 tbl] 1 (3: 5) times, k2.

3rd row P2, [Tw2, p2] 1 (3: 5) times, C4F, work 3rd row of panel A, C4F, work 3rd row of panel B, C4F, work 3rd row of panel C, C4B, work 3rd row of panel B, C4B, work 3rd row of panel A, C4B, [p2, Tw2] 1 (3: 5) times, p2.

4th row K2, [p2 tbl, k2] 1 (3: 5) times, p4, work 4th row of panel A, p4, work 4th row of panel B, p4, work 4th row of panel C, p4, work 4th row of panel B, p4, work 4th row of panel A, p4, [k2, p2 tbl] 1 (3: 5) times, k2.

These 4 rows set position of panels, form cable patt between panels and twisted rib patt at side edges. Cont in patt until Back measures approximately 52 (57: 62)cm/ 20 ½ (22 ½: 24 ½)in from beg, ending with 28th (14th: 28th) row of panel C patt.

Shape Shoulders

Cast off 22 (25: 29) sts at beg of next 2 rows and 21 (25: 28) sts at beg of 2 foll rows.

Leave rem 46 (48: 50) sts on a holder.

FRONT

Work as given for Back until Front measures approximately 44 (49: 54)cm/ 17 ½ (19 ½: 21 ½)in from beg, ending with 6th (20th: 6th) row of panel C patt.

Shape Neck

Next row Patt 50 (58: 66), turn.
Work on this set of sts only.
Keeping patt correct, dec one st at neck edge on next 4 rows then on every alt row until 43 (50: 57) sts rem. Cont straight until Front matches Back to shoulder shaping, ending at side edge.

Shape Shoulder

Cast off 22 (25: 29) sts at beg of next row.
Work 1 row. Cast off rem 21 (25: 28) sts.
With right side facing, slip center 32 sts onto a holder, rejoin yarn to rem sts and patt to end.
Complete to match first side.

SLEEVES

With 3 ¼mm (No 10/US 3) needles, cast on 47 (49: 51) sts.
Beg with a k row, work 5 rows in st st.
Next row P7 (8: 9), [m1, p8] 5 times, p0 (1: 2). 52 (54: 56) sts.
Change to 4mm (No 8/US 6) needles.
1st row (right side) P0 (1: 2), [Tw2, p2] twice, k4, work 1st row of panel C, k4, [p2, Tw2] twice, p0 (1: 2).
2nd row K0 (1: 2), [p2 tbl, k2] twice, p4, work 2nd row of panel C, p4, [k2, p2 tbl] twice, k0 (1: 2).
3rd row P0 (1: 2), [Tw2, p2] twice, C4F, work 3rd row of panel C, C4B, [p2, Tw2] twice, p0 (1: 2).
4th row K0 (1: 2), [p2 tbl, k2] twice, p4, work 4th row of panel C, p4, [k2, p2 tbl] twice, k0 (1: 2).
These 4 rows set position of panel, form cable patt at each side of panel and twisted rib patt at side edges.
Cont in patt, inc one st at each end of next row and 13 foll 3rd rows, then on every foll 4th row until 98 (104: 108) sts, working inc sts into twisted rib patt. Cont straight until Sleeve measures 35 (37: 39)cm/13 ¾ (14 ½: 15 ½)in from beg, ending with a wrong side row.
Cast off.

NECKBAND

Join right shoulder seam.

1st and 3rd sizes only

With 3 ¼mm (No 10/US 3) needles and right side facing, k up 25 sts down left front neck, work across center front sts as follows:
[p1, k1 tbl] 3 times, p3 tog, [k1 tbl, p1] 3 times, k2 tog tbl, [p1, k1 tbl] 3 times, p3 tog, [k1 tbl, p1] 3 times, k up 24 sts up right front neck, work across back neck sts as follows:
[k1 tbl, p1] 1 (2) times, k2 tog tbl, p1, k1 tbl, p2 tog, [k1 tbl, p1] 4 times, k2 tog tbl, [p1, k1 tbl] twice, p2 tog, [k1 tbl, p1] twice, k2 tog tbl, [p1, k1 tbl] 4 times, p2 tog, [k1 tbl, p1] 3 (4) times. 116 (120) sts.

2nd size only

With 3 ¼mm (No 10/US 3) needles and right side facing, k up 25 sts down left front neck, work across center front sts as follows:
p1, [k1 tbl, p1] twice, k2 tog tbl, [p1, k1 tbl] 4 times, p2 tog, [k1 tbl, p1] 4 times, k2 tog tbl, [p1, k1 tbl] twice, p1, k up 24 sts up right front neck, work across back neck sts as follows:
[k1 tbl, p2 tog] 3 times, [k1 tbl, p1] 5 times, k3 tog tbl, p1, k2 tog tbl, p1, k3 tog tbl, [p1, k1 tbl] 5 times, p2 tog, k1 tbl, p1, k1 tbl, p2 tog, k1 tbl, p1. 116 sts.

All sizes

1st rib row [K1, p1 tbl] to end.
2nd rib row [K1 tbl, p1] to end.
Rib a further 3 rows. Beg with a k row, work 6 rows in st st.
Cast off loosely.

TO MAKE UP

Join left shoulder and neckband seam, reversing seam on st st section of neckband. Sew in sleeves, placing center of sleeves to shoulder seams. Join side and sleeve seams, reversing seams on first and last six rows.

Cable and Garter-stitch Sweater

MATERIALS
15 (17) 50g balls of Rowan DK Handknit Cotton.
Pair each of 3 ¼mm (No 10/US 3) and 4mm (No 8/US 6) knitting needles.
Cable needle.

TENSION
20 sts and 28 rows to 10cm/4in square over st st on 4mm (No 8/US 6) needles.

ABBREVIATIONS
See page 8.

PANEL A
Worked over 16 sts.
1st row (right side) P2, k2, p2, k4, p2, k2, p2.
2nd row K2, p2, k2, p4, k2, p2, k2.
3rd to 8th rows Rep 1st and 2nd rows 3 times.
9th row P2, sl next 4 sts onto cable needle and leave at back of work, k2, then p2, k2, from cable needle, sl next 2 sts onto cable needle and leave at front of work, k2, p2, then k2 from cable needle, p2.
10th row As 2nd row.
11th to 14th rows Rep 1st and 2nd rows twice.
15th row As 1st row.
16th to 20th rows K16.
These 20 rows form patt.

PANEL B
Worked over 14 sts.
1st row (right side) K4, [p1, k4] twice.
2nd row K5, p4, k5.
3rd row K4, p1, sl next 2 sts onto cable needle and leave at front of work, k2, then k2 from cable needle, p1, k4.
4th row As 2nd row.
5th and 6th rows As 1st and 2nd rows.
These 6 rows form patt.

MEASUREMENTS

To fit age	4-6	8-10	years
Actual chest measurement	92 36	116 45 ½	cm in
Length	50 19 ¾	58 23	cm in
Sleeve seam	32 12 ½	37 14 ½	cm in

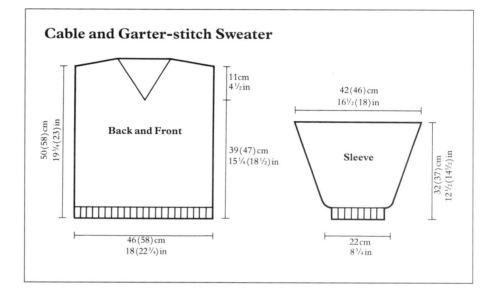

Cable and Garter-stitch Sweater

Back and Front

11cm 4½in

39 (47) cm 15¼ (18½) in

50 (58) cm 19¼ (23) in

46 (58) cm 18 (22¾) in

42 (46) cm 16½ (18) in

Sleeve

32 (37) cm 12½ (14½) in

22 cm 8¾ in

BACK
With 3 ¼mm (No 10/US 3) needles cast on 92 (116) sts.
1st rib row (right side) P1, k2, [p2, k2] to last st, p1.
2nd rib row K1, p2, [k2, p2] to last st, k1.
Rib a further 5 rows.
Inc row Rib 2, [m1, rib 7, m1, rib 2, m1, rib 7, m1, rib 3, m1, rib 2, m1, rib 3] to last 18 sts, [m1, rib 7, m1, rib 2] twice. 114 (144) sts.
Change to 4mm (No 8/US 6) needles.
1st row (right side) K4, work 1st row of panel A, [work 1st row of panel B, then panel A] to last 4 sts, k4.
The last row sets position of panels and forms garter st at side edges. Cont in patt until Back measures 50 (58)cm/19 ¾ (23)in from beg, ending with a wrong side row.

Shape Shoulders
Cast off 20 (26) sts at beg of next 2 rows and 20 (27) sts at beg of foll 2 rows. Leave rem 34 (38) sts on a holder.

FRONT
Work as given for Back until Front measures 39 (47)cm/15 ¼ (18 ½)in from beg, ending with a wrong side row.

Shape Neck
Next row Patt 55 (70), turn.
Work on this set of sts only. Dec one st at neck edge on next 4 rows then on every foll alt row until 40 (53) sts rem. Cont straight until Front matches Back to shoulder shaping, ending at side edge.

Shape Shoulder
Cast off 20 (26) sts at beg of next row.
Work 1 row. Cast off rem 20 (27) sts.
With right side facing, slip center 4 sts onto a safety pin, rejoin yarn to rem sts, patt to end. Complete to match first side.

SLEEVES
With 3 ¼mm (No 10/US 3) needles cast on 44 sts.
Work 15 rows in rib as given for Back welt.
Inc row [Rib 2, m1, rib 7, m1] twice, rib 3, m1, rib 2, m1, rib 3, [m1, rib 7, m1, rib 2] twice. 54 sts.
Change to 4mm (No 8/US 6) needles.
1st row (right side) K4, work 1st row of panel A, then panel B and panel A, k4.
This row sets position of panels.
Cont in patt, inc one st at each end of 10 foll alt rows, working inc sts into panel B patt. 74 sts.
Now inc one st at each end of every foll 4th row until there are 98 (106) sts, working inc sts into garter st.
Cont straight until Sleeve measures 32 (37)cm/12 ½ (14 ½)in from beg, ending with a wrong side row.
Cast off.

NECKBAND
Join right shoulder seam.
With 3 ¼mm (No 10/US 3) needles and right side facing, k up 34 sts down left front neck, [k2 tog] twice across sts on safety pin (mark these 2 sts), k up 34 sts up right front neck, k back neck sts. 104 (108) sts.
1st rib row P2, [k2, p2] to 2 sts before marked sts, k2 tog tbl, p2, k2 tog, [p2, k2] to end.
2nd rib row P2, [k2, p2] to 3 sts before marked sts, k1, k2 tog tbl, k2, k2 tog, k1, [p2, k2] to end.
3rd rib row Rib to 2 sts before marked sts, p2 tog tbl, p2, p2 tog, rib to end.
4th row Rib to 2 sts before marked sts, p2 tog tbl, k2, p2 tog, rib to end.
5th row Rib to 2 sts before marked sts, k2 tog tbl, p2, k2 tog, rib to end.
Cast off in rib, dec one st at each side of marked sts as before.

TO MAKE UP
Join left shoulder and neckband seam. Sew on sleeves, placing center of sleeves to shoulder seams. Join side and sleeve seams.

Moss and Cable Jacket with Petal Collar

MATERIALS
10 (11: 14) 50g balls of Rowan DK Handknit Cotton.
Pair each of 3 ¼mm (No 10/US 3) and 4mm (No 8/US 6) knitting needles.
Cable needle.
7 buttons.

TENSION
22 sts and 32 rows to 10cm/4in square over pattern on 4mm (No 8/US 6) needles.

ABBREVIATIONS
See page 8.

PANEL A
Worked over 4 sts.
1st row (right side) K4.
2nd row P4.
3rd row Sl next 2 sts onto cable needle and leave at front of work, k2, then k2 from cable needle.
4th row P4.
5th and 6th rows As 1st and 2nd rows.
These 6 rows form patt.

PANEL B
Worked over 7 sts.
1st row (right side) K1, p1, k5.
2nd row P4, k1, p2.
3rd row [K1, p1] twice, k3.
4th row P2, k1, p1, k1, p2.
5th row [K1, p1] 3 times, k1.
6th row As 4th row.
7th row As 3rd row.
8th row As 2nd row.
9th row As 1st row.
10th row P7.
These 10 rows form patt.

PANEL C
Worked over 7 sts.
1st row (right side) K5, p1, k1.
2nd row P2, k1, p4.
3rd row K3, [p1, k1] twice.
4th row P2, k1, p1, k1, p2.
5th row K1, [p1, k1] 3 times.
6th row As 4th row.
7th row As 3rd row.
8th row As 2nd row.
9th row As 1st row.
10th row P7.
These 10 rows form patt.

MEASUREMENTS

To fit age	2-4	4-6	6–8	years
Actual chest	72	85	102	cm
measurement	28 ½	33 ½	40	in
Length	43	50	58	cm
	17	19 ¾	23	in
Sleeve seam	26	31	38	cm
	10 ¼	12 ¼	15	in

Moss and Cable Jacket with Petal Collar

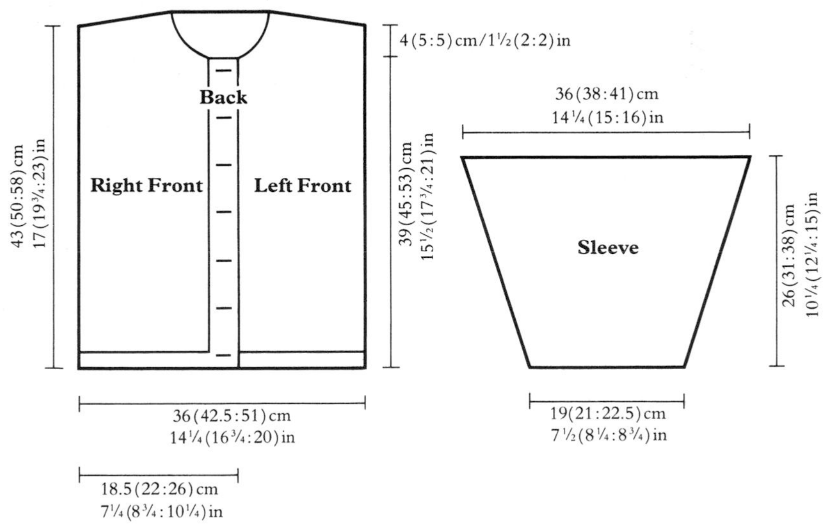

4(5:5)cm/1½(2:2)in
Back
Right Front
Left Front
43(50:58)cm
17(19¾:23)in
39(45:53)cm
15½(17¾:21)in
36(42.5:51)cm
14¼(16¾:20)in
18.5(22:26)cm
7¼(8¾:10¼)in
36(38:41)cm
14¼(15:16)in
Sleeve
26(31:38)cm
10¼(12¼:15)in
19(21:22.5)cm
7½(8¼:8¾)in

BACK

With 3 ¼mm (No 10/US 3) needles cast on 75 (89: 105) sts.
1st row K1 (0: 0), [p1, k1] to last 0 (1: 1) st, p0 (1: 1).
This row forms moss st. Moss st 2 rows more.
Next row Moss st 5 (12: 4), [m1, moss st 16] 4 (4: 6) times, m1, moss st to end. 80 (94: 112) sts.
Change to 4mm (No 8/US 6) needles.
1st row (right side) Moss st 1 (1: 0), [work 1st row of panel B] 0 (1: 0) time, [moss st 3, work 1st row of panel A, moss st 3, work 1st row of panel B] 2 (2: 3) times, moss st 3, work 1st row of panel A, moss st 3, [work 1st row of panel C, moss st 3, work 1st row of panel A, moss st 3] 2 (2: 3) times, [work 1st row of panel C] 0 (1: 0) time, moss st 1 (1: 0).
2nd row Moss st 1 (1: 0), [work 2nd row of panel C] 0 (1: 0) time, [moss st 3, work 2nd row of panel A, moss st 3, work 2nd row of panel C] 2 (2: 3) times, moss st 3, work 2nd row of panel A, moss st 3, [work 2nd row of panel B, moss st 3, work 2nd row of panel A, moss st 3] 2 (2: 3) times, [work 2nd row of panel B] 0 (1: 0) time, moss st 1 (1: 0).
These 2 rows set position of panels. Cont in patt until Back measures 43 (50: 58)cm/17 (19 ¾: 23)in from beg, ending with a wrong side row.

Shape Shoulders

Cast off 11 (14: 18) sts at beg of next 2 rows and 12 (15: 19) sts at beg of foll 2 rows.
Leave rem 34 (36: 38) sts on a holder.

LEFT FRONT

With 3 ¼mm (No 10/US 3) needles, cast on 39 (46: 54) sts.
1st row K1 (0: 0), [p1, k1] to end.
2nd row [K1, p1] to last 1 (0: 0) st, k1 (0: 0).
These 2 rows form moss st. Moss st 1 row.
Next row Moss st 17, [m1, moss st 16] 1 (1: 2) times, m1, moss st to end. 41 (48: 57) sts.
Change to 4mm (No 8/US 6) needles.
1st row (right side) Moss st 1 (1: 0), [work 1st row of panel B] 0 (1: 0) time, [moss st 3, work 1st row of panel A, moss st 3, work 1st row of panel B] 2 (2: 3) times, moss st 6.
2nd row Moss st 6, [work 2nd row of panel B, moss st 3, work 2nd row of panel A, moss st 3] 2 (2: 3) times, [work 2nd row of panel B] 0 (1: 0) time, moss st 1 (1: 0).
These 2 rows set position of panels. Cont in patt until Front measures 39 (45: 53)cm/ 15 ½ (17 ½: 21)in from beg, ending with a wrong side row.

Shape Neck

Next row Patt to last 6 sts, turn; leave the 6 sts on a safety pin.
Keeping patt correct, work 1 row.
Cast off 5 sts at beg of next row. Dec one st at neck edge on every row until 23 (29: 37) sts rem.
Cont straight until Front matches Back to shoulder shaping, ending with a wrong side row.

Shape Shoulder

Cast off 11 (14: 18) sts at beg of next row.
Work 1 row. Cast off rem 12 (15: 19) sts.
Mark front edge to indicate position of 7 buttons: first one 4 rows up from lower edge, last one 2 rows below neck shaping and rem 5 evenly spaced between.

RIGHT FRONT

With 3 ¼mm (No 10/US 3) needles cast on 39 (46: 54) sts.
1st row [K1, p1] to last 1 (0: 0) st, k1 (0: 0).
2nd row K1 (0: 0), [p1, k1] to end.
These 2 rows form moss st. Moss st 1 row more.
Next row Moss st 5 (12: 4), [m1, moss st 16] 2 (2: 3) times, moss st 2. 41 (48: 57) sts.
Change to 4mm (No 8/US 6) needles.
1st (buttonhole) row (right side) Moss st 2, k2 tog, yf, moss st 2, [work 1st row of panel C, moss st 3, work 1st row of panel A, moss st 3] 2 (2: 3) times, [work 1st row of panel C] 0 (1: 0) time, moss st 1 (1: 0).
2nd row Moss st 1 (1: 0), [work 2nd row of panel C] 0 (1: 0) time, [moss st 3, work 2nd row of panel A, moss st 3, work 2nd row of panel C] 2 (2: 3) times, moss st 6.
These 2 rows set position of panels.
Complete to match Left Front, making buttonholes to match markers and reversing shapings.

SLEEVES

With 3 ¼mm (No 10/US 3) needles cast on 39 (43: 47) sts.
Work 3 rows in moss st patt as given for 1st size on Back.
Next row Moss st 3 (5: 7), [m1, moss st 16] twice, m1, moss st to end. 42 (46: 50) sts.
Change to 4mm (No 8/US 6) needles.
1st row (right side) Moss st 2 (4: 6), work 1st row of panel A, moss st 3, work 1st row of panel B, moss st 3, work 1st row of panel A, moss st 3, work 1st row of panel C, moss st 3, work 1st row of panel A, moss st 2 (4: 6).
2nd row Moss st 2 (4: 6), work 2nd row of panel A, moss st 3, work 2nd row of panel C, moss st 3, work 2nd row of panel A, moss st 3, work 2nd row of panel B, moss st 3, work 2nd row of panel A, moss st 2 (4: 6).
These 2 rows set position of panels. Cont in patt, inc one st at each end of 3rd row and every foll 3rd (4th: 5th) row until there are 80 (84: 90) sts, working inc sts into moss st.
Cont straight until Sleeve measures 26 (31: 38)cm/10 ¼ (12 ¼: 15)in from beg, ending with a wrong side row.
Cast off.

COLLAR

Join shoulder seams.

With 3 ¼mm (No 10/US 3) needles and right side facing, slip 6 sts from right front safety pin onto needle, k up 18 (21: 21) sts up right front neck, work across back neck as follows: k0 (1: 0), [k2 tog] 1 (1: 2) times, moss st 5, work 3 tog, moss st 5, k1, k2 tog, k1, moss st 5, work 3 tog, moss st 5, [k2 tog] 1 (1: 2) times, k0 (1: 0), k up 18 (21: 21) sts down left front neck, moss st 6 sts from left front safety pin. 75 (83: 83) sts.

Cont in moss st, work 1 row. Cast off 3 sts at beg of next 2 rows. 69 (77: 77) sts.

Next row Moss st 4 (3: 3), work into front, back and front of next st, [moss st 5 (6: 6), work into front, back and front of next st] 10 times, moss st to end. 91 (99: 99) sts. Moss st 6 rows.

**Next row Moss st 9 and turn.

Work on these 9 sts only. Dec one st at each end of next row and 2 foll alt rows.

Patt 1 row. Work 3 tog and fasten off. Rejoin yarn to rem sts and rep from ** until all sts are worked off and dec one st at beg of making 6th point on **1st size only**.

TO MAKE UP

Sew on sleeves, placing center of sleeves to shoulder seams. Join side and sleeve seams. Sew on buttons.

Right: Cabled Tunic with Shawl Collar (see page 79) and Moss and Cable Jacket with Petal Collar.

Fair Isle Sweater with Two-color Rib

MATERIALS

5 (6: 7) 50g balls of Rowan DK Handknit
Cotton in Maroon (A).
3 (4: 5) balls of same in Black (B).
2 (2: 3) balls of same in Green.
1 ball of same in each of Pink, Blue, Lime,
Lilac and White.
Pair each of 3 ¼mm (No 10/US 3) and
4mm (No 8/US 6) knitting needles.

TENSION

22 sts and 25 rows to 10cm/4in square over
pattern on 4mm (No 8/US 6) needles.

ABBREVIATIONS

See page 8.

NOTES

Read chart from right to left on right side
(k) rows and from left to right on wrong
side (p) rows. When working in rib or
pattern, strand yarn not in use loosely
across wrong side over no more than 5 sts at
a time to keep fabric elastic.

MEASUREMENTS

To fit age	5-7	7–9	9-11	years
Actual chest measurement	90	100	112	cm
	35 ½	39 ½	44	in
Length	45	53	57	cm
	17 ¾	21	22 ½	in
Sleeve seam	31	36	41	cm
	12 ¼	14 ¼	16	in

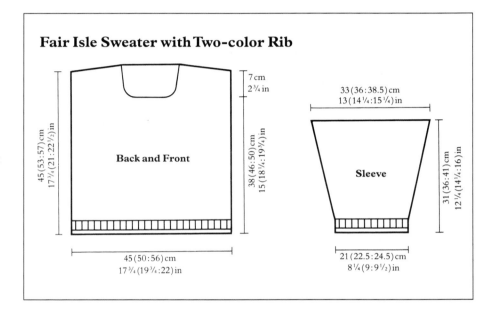

Fair Isle Sweater with Two-color Rib

Back and Front

45(53:57)cm
17¾(21:22½)in

7cm
2¾in

38(46:50)cm
15(18¼:19¾)in

45(50:56)cm
17¾(19¾:22)in

33(36:38.5)cm
13(14¼:15¼)in

Sleeve

31(36:41)cm
12¼(14¼:16)in

21(22.5:24.5)cm
8¼(9:9½)in

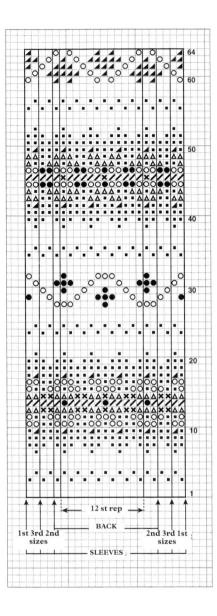

1st 3rd 2nd sizes
BACK
2nd 3rd 1st sizes
12 st rep
SLEEVES

KEY

□ Maroon (A)
▪ Black (B)
◙ Green
◢ Pink
△ Blue
✕ Lime
● Lilac
◿ White

BACK

With 3 ¼mm (No 10/US 3) needles and A, cast on 98 (110: 122) sts.
Beg with a k row, work 4 rows in st st.
1st rib row (right side) P2A, [k2B, p2A] to end.
2nd rib row K2A, [p2B, k2A] to end.
Rep last 2 rows twice more, inc one st at center of last row. 99 (111: 123) sts.
Change to 4mm (No 8/US 6) needles.
Beg with a k row, work in st st and patt from chart until Back measures 45 (53: 57)cm/17 ¾ (21: 22 ½)in from beg, ending with a wrong side row.

Shape Shoulders

Cast off 16 (18: 20) sts at beg of next 4 rows.
Leave rem 35 (39: 43) sts on a holder.

FRONT

Work as given for Back until Front measures 38 (46: 50)cm/15 (18 ¼: 19 ¾)in from beg, ending with a wrong side row.

Shape Neck

Next row Patt 40 (44: 48), turn.
Work on this set of sts only. Keeping patt correct, dec one st at neck edge on next 4 rows, then on 4 foll alt rows. 32 (36: 40) sts.
Cont straight until Front matches Back to shoulder shaping, ending at side edge.

Shape Shoulder

Cast off 16 (18: 20) sts at beg of next row.
Work 1 row. Cast off rem 16 (18: 20) sts.
With right side facing, slip center 19 (23: 27) sts onto holder, rejoin yarn to rem sts, patt to end.
Complete to match first side of neck.

SLEEVES

With 3 ¼mm (No 10/US 3) needles and A, cast on 46 (50: 54) sts.
Beg with a k row, work 4 rows in st st, then 4 rows in rib as given for Back, inc one st at center of last row. 47 (51: 55) sts.
Change to 4mm (No 8/US 6) needles.
Beg with a k row, work in st st and patt from chart, at the same time, inc one st at each end of 3rd row and every foll 4th (5th: 6th) row until there are 73 (79: 85) sts, working inc sts into patt.
Cont straight until Sleeve measures 31 (36: 41)cm/12 ¼ (14 ¼: 16)in from beg, ending with a wrong side row.
Cast off.

NECKBAND

Join right shoulder seam.
With 3 ¼mm (No 10/US 3) needles, A and right side facing, k up 16 sts down left front neck, k center front neck sts, k up 16 sts up right front neck, k back neck sts. 86 (94: 102) sts.
Beg with a 2nd row, work 4 rows in rib as given for Back.
Cont in A only. Beg with a p row, work 4 rows in st st.
Cast off loosely.

TO MAKE UP

Join left shoulder and neckband seam, reversing seam on st st section of neckband.
Sew on sleeves, placing center of sleeves to shoulder seams.
Join side and sleeve seams, reversing seams on first and last 4 rows.

Right: Fair Isle Sweater with Two-color Rib, Aran Sweater (see page 63), Moss and Cable Jacket with Petal Collar (see page 71), Cable and Garter-stitch Sweater (see page 67), and Cabled Tunic with Shawl Collar (see page 79).

Cabled Tunic with Shawl Collar

MATERIALS
11 (12: 14) 50g balls of Rowan Cotton Glace.
Pair each of 3mm (No 11/US 2) and 3 ¼mm (No 10/US 3) knitting needles.
One 3 ¼mm (No 10/US 3) circular needle.
Cable needle.

TENSION
28 sts and 40 rows to 10cm/4in square over pattern on 3 ¼mm (No 10/US 3) needles.

ABBREVIATIONS
C4B = sl next 2 sts onto cable needle and leave at back of work, k2, then k2 from cable needle;
Cr3L = sl next 2 sts onto cable needle and leave at front of work, p1, then k2 from cable needle;
Cr3R = sl next st onto cable needle and leave at back of work, k2, then p1 from cable needle;
mb = p into front, back, front, back, front, then k into back of next st, pass 2nd, 3rd, 4th, 5th and 6th st over 1st st.
Also see page 8.

PANEL A
Worked over 7 sts.
1st row (right side) P7.
2nd row P7.
3rd row P3, mb, p3.
4th, 5th and 6th rows P7.
These 6 rows form patt.

MEASUREMENTS

To fit age	3-4	6–8	8-10	years
Actual chest measurement	80 31 ½	95 37 ½	110 43 ½	cm in
Length	45 17 ¾	52 20 ½	61 24	cm in
Sleeve seam	29 11 ½	34 13 ½	40 15 ¾	cm in

Cabled Tunic with Shawl Collar

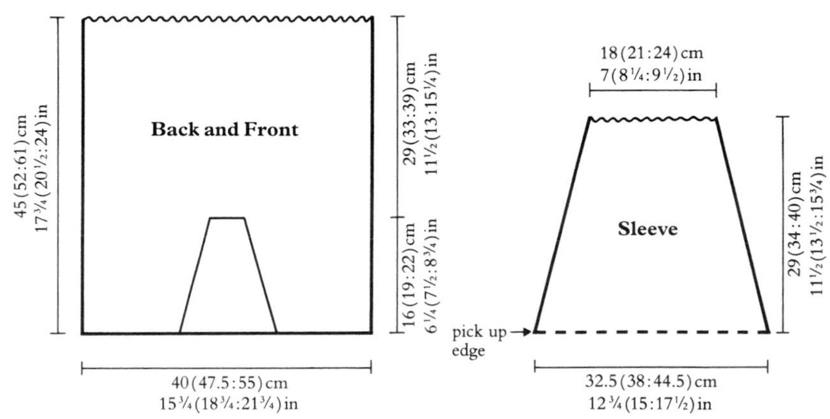
Back and Front
45 (52:61) cm
17¾ (20½:24) in
29 (33:39) cm
11½ (13:15¼) in
16 (19:22) cm
6¼ (7½:8¾) in
40 (47.5:55) cm
15¾ (18¾:21¾) in
18 (21:24) cm
7 (8¼:9½) in
Sleeve
29 (34:40) cm
11½ (13½:15¾) in
pick up edge
32.5 (38:44.5) cm
12¾ (15:17½) in

PANEL B
Worked over 14 sts.
1st row (right side) P5, C4B, p5.
2nd row K5, p4, k5.
3rd row P4, Cr3R, Cr3L, p4.
4th row K4, p6, k4.
5th row P3, Cr3R, p2, Cr3L, p3.
6th row K3, p8, k3.
7th row P2, Cr3R, p4, Cr3L, p2.
8th row K2, p10, k2.
9th row P1, Cr3R, p6, Cr3L, p1.
10th row K1, p12, k1.
11th row P1, Cr3L, p6, Cr3R, p1.
12th row As 8th row.
13th row P2, Cr3L, p4, Cr3R, p2.
14th row As 6th row.
15th row P3, Cr3L, p2, Cr3R, p3.
16th row As 4th row.
17th row P4, Cr3L, Cr3R, p4.
18th row As 2nd row.
19th and 20th rows As 1st and 2nd rows.
21st row P5, k4, p5.
22nd row As 2nd row.
These 22 rows form patt.

BACK

Begin at shoulders.

With 3 ¼mm (No 10/US 3) needles cast on 112 (133, 154) sts.

1st row (right side) Work 1st row of panel A, [work 1st row of panel B, then panel A] to end.

This row sets position of panels.

Cont in patt until Back measures approximately 43 (50: 59)cm/17 (19 ¾: 23 ¼)in from beg, ending with 19th (1st: 19th) row of panel B.

P 1 row, dec 2 sts over each cable. 102 (121: 140) sts.

Change to 3mm (No 11/US 2) needles.

P 5 rows.

Next row P2 (3: 3), [p2 tog, p4] to last 4 (4: 5) sts, p2 tog, p2 (2: 3). 85 (101: 117) sts.

Next row Cast off purlwise 2 sts, [sl st used in casting off back onto left hand needle, cast on 2 sts purlwise, cast off 4 sts purlwise] to end.

Fasten off.

FRONT

Begin at left shoulder.

With 3 ¼mm (No 10/US 3) needles cast on 38 (46: 54) sts.

1st size only

1st row (right side) P1, C4B, p5, work 1st row of panel A, then panel B and panel A.

2nd row Work 2nd row of panel A, then panel B and panel A, k5, p4, k1.

2nd size only

1st row (right side) P4, [work 1st row of panel B, then panel A] twice.

2nd row [Work 2nd row of panel A, then panel B] twice, p4.

3rd size only

1st row (right side) P5, work 1st row of panel A, [work 1st row of panel B, then panel A] twice.

2nd row [Work 2nd row of panel A, then panel B] twice, work 2nd row of panel A, k5.

All sizes

These 2 rows set position of panels.

Cont in patt, inc one st at beg of 5th row and at same edge on every foll 7th row until there are 46 (56: 66) sts, working inc sts into patt.

Patt 8 (6: 4) rows straight. Leave these sts on a spare needle.

With 3 ¼mm (No 10/US 3) needles cast on 38 (46: 54) sts for right side of neck.

1st size only

1st row (right side) Work 1st row of panel A, then panel B and panel A, p5, C4B, p1.

2nd row K1, p4, k5, work 2nd row of panel A, then panel B and panel A.

2nd size only

1st row (right side) [Work 1st row of panel A, then panel B] twice, p4.

2nd row P4, [work 2nd row of panel B, then panel A] twice.

3rd size only

1st row (right side) Work 1st row of panel A [work 1st row of panel B, then panel A] twice, p5.

2nd row K5, work 2nd row of panel A, [work 2nd row of panel B, then panel A] twice.

All sizes

These 2 rows set position of panels.

Cont in patt, inc one st at end of 5th row and at same edge on every foll 7th row until there are 46 (56: 66) sts, working inc sts into patt.

Patt 8 (6: 4) rows straight.

Next row Patt to end, cast on 20 (21: 22) sts, then patt across sts on spare needle. 112 (133: 154) sts.

Mark each end of last row. Complete as given for Back.

SLEEVES

Join shoulder seams.

Mark same row at side edges of Back as on Front.

With 3 ¼mm (No 10/US 3) needles and right side facing, k up 91 (106: 125) sts between markers.

1st row (wrong side) P7 (4: 3), work 22nd row of panel B, [work 6th row of panel A, work 22nd row of panel B] to last 7 (4: 3) sts, p7 (4: 3).

2nd row P7 (4: 3), work 1st row of panel B, [work 1st row of panel A, then panel B] to last 7 (4: 3) sts, p7 (4: 3).

These 2 rows set position of panels.

Cont in patt, dec one st at each end of 9th (9th: 7th) row, then every foll 5th row until 51 (58: 67) sts rem.

Patt 2 (4: 3) rows straight.

1st size only

Next row P7, *p2 tog, p4, [p2 tog] twice, p4, p2 tog, p5; rep from * once more, p2.

2nd and 3rd sizes only

Next row [P2 tog, p4] 1 (0) time, **[p2 tog] twice, p4, p2 tog, p5, p2 tog, p4; rep from ** 1 (2) times more, [p2 tog] twice, p6 (0).

All sizes

43 (47: 53) sts.

Change to 3mm (No 11/US 2) needles.

P5 rows.

Next row P3 (5: 3), [p2 tog, p3] to last 5 (7: 5) sts, p2 tog, p3 (5: 3). 35 (39: 43) sts.

Cast off as given for Back.

COLLAR

With 3 ¼mm (No 10/US 3) circular needle and right side facing, k up 47 (56: 65) sts up right front neck, 32 (36: 42) sts across back neck and 47 (56: 65) sts down left front neck. 126 (148: 172) sts.

Work backwards and forwards in rows. K 27 (29: 31) rows, dec 5 (7: 9) sts evenly across last row. 121 (141: 163) sts.

Next row Cast off knitwise 2 sts, [sl st used in casting off back onto left hand needle, cast on 2 sts knitwise, cast off 4 sts knitwise] to end.

Fasten off.

TO MAKE UP

Beginning 6cm/2 ¼in up from lower edge, join side seams, then sleeve seams. Lap right side of collar over left side and catch down row ends of collar together to cast on sts at center of front.

Shawl-collared Jacket with Fair Isle Bands

MATERIALS
3 (4: 6: 7: 8) 50g balls of Rowan Cotton Glace in Cream (A).
1 (1: 2: 2: 2) balls of same in Beige.
1 (1: 1: 2: 2) balls of same in Pink.
1 (1: 1: 1: 2) balls of same in Light Blue.
Pair each of 3mm (No 11/US 2) and 3 ¼mm (No 10/US 3) knitting needles.
8 (8: 9: 9: 10) buttons.

TENSION
26 sts and 33 rows to 10cm/4in square over pattern on 3 ¼mm (No 10/US 3) needles.

ABBREVIATIONS
See page 8.

NOTES
Read chart from right to left on right side (k) rows and from left to right on wrong side (p) rows. When working in pattern, strand yarn not in use loosely across wrong side of work to keep fabric elastic.

BACK AND FRONTS
Worked in one piece to armholes.
With 3mm (No 11/US 2) needles and A, cast on 155 (175: 195: 215: 235) sts.
Next row K1, [p1, k1] to end.
This row forms moss st. 1 row.
Buttonhole row Moss st 2, yrn, p2 tog, patt to end.
Moss st 1 row.
Next row Moss st 5 and sl these 5 sts onto safety pin, moss st to last 5 sts, sl last 5 sts onto safety pin. 145 (165: 185: 205: 225) sts.
Change to 3 ¼mm (No 10/US 3) needles.
Beg with a p row, cont in st st and patt from chart until work measures 17 (19: 21: 23: 27)cm/6 ¾ (7 ½: 8 ¼: 9: 10 ½)in from beg, ending with a wrong side row.

Right Front
Next row Patt 35 (40: 45: 50: 55), turn.
Work on this set of sts only.

MEASUREMENTS

To fit age	1	2	3-4	4-6	6-8	years
Actual chest measurement	58	65	73	80	88	cm
	22 ¾	25 ½	28 ¾	31 ½	34 ½	in
Length	29	33	36	40	45	cm
	11 ½	13	14 ¼	15 ¾	17 ¾	in
Sleeve seam	19	23	28	32	38	cm
	7 ½	9	11	12 ½	15	in

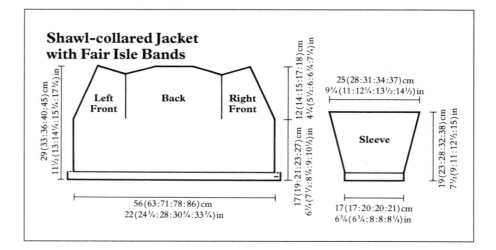

Shawl-collared Jacket with Fair Isle Bands

Left Front   Back   Right Front

29(33:36:40:45)cm
11½(13:14¼:15¾:17¾)in

12(14:15:17:18)cm
4¾(5½:6:6¾:7¼)in

17(19:21:23:27)cm
6¾(7½:8¼:9:10½)in

56(63:71:78:86)cm
22(24¾:28:30¾:33¾)in

25(28:31:34:37)cm
9¾(11:12¼:13½:14½)in

Sleeve

19(23:28:32:38)cm
7½(9:11:12½:15)in

17(17:20:20:21)cm
6¾(6¾:8:8:8¼)in

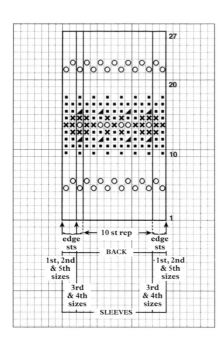

KEY

☐ Cream (A)
▣ Beige
◎ Pink
☒ Light Blue
◪ Dark Blue

Shape Neck

Keeping patt correct, dec one st at neck edge on every 3rd row until 24 (28: 32: 36: 40) sts rem. Cont straight until Front measures 29 (33: 36: 40: 45)cm/11 ½(13: 14 ¼: 15 ¾: 17 ¾)in from beg, ending at armhole edge.

Shape Shoulder

Cast off 12 (14: 16: 18: 20) sts at beg of next row.
Work 1 row. Cast off rem 12 (14: 16: 18: 20) sts.

Back

With right side facing, rejoin yarn to rem sts, patt 75 (85: 95: 105: 115) sts, turn. Work straight on this set of sts only until Back matches Front to shoulder shaping, ending with a wrong side row.

Shape Shoulders

Cast off 12 (14: 16: 18: 20) sts at beg of next 4 rows.
Leave rem 27 (29: 31: 33: 35) sts on a holder.

Left Front

With right side facing, rejoin yarn to rem sts and patt to end.
Complete as given for Right Front.

SLEEVES

With 3mm (No 11/US 2) needles and A, cast on 35 (37: 39: 41: 43) sts.
Work 4 rows in moss st.
Next row Moss st 4 (4: 3: 2: 5), m1, [moss st 3 (4: 3: 4: 3), m1] to last 4 (5: 3: 3: 5) sts, moss st to end. 45 (45: 51: 51: 55) sts.
Change to 3 ¼mm (No 10/US 3) needles.
Beg with a p row, work in st st and patt from chart, at the same time, inc one st at each end of 3rd row and every foll 4th (4th: 5th: 4th: 5th) row until there are 65 (73: 81: 89: 97) sts, working inc sts into patt.
Cont straight until Sleeve measures 19 (23: 28: 32: 38)cm/7 ½ (9: 11: 12 ½: 15)in from beg, ending with a wrong side row.
Cast off.

BUTTON BAND AND LEFT COLLAR

With 3mm (No 11/US 2) needles, rejoin A yarn at inside edge to 5 sts on left front safety pin, inc in first st, moss st to end. Cont in moss st until band, when slightly stretched, fits up left front to beg of neck shaping.

Shape Collar

Inc and work into moss st, one st at inside edge on next row and every foll 4th row until there are 15 sts.
Cont straight until collar fits left front neck to shoulder, ending at outside edge.
Next 2 rows Moss st 9, turn, sl 1, moss st to end.
Moss st 6 rows.
Rep last 8 rows until collar fits left front neck to center of back neck.
Cast off.
Mark band to indicate position of 4 (4: 5: 5: 6) buttons: first one to match buttonhole already made on right front welt, last one 2 rows below collar shaping and rem 2 (2: 3: 3: 4) evenly spaced between.

BUTTONHOLE BAND AND RIGHT COLLAR

Work as given for Button Band and Left Collar, making buttonholes to match markers as before.

SIDE BELTS (make 2)

With 3mm (No 11/US 2) needles and A, cast on 7 sts.
Work in moss st for 8 (8: 9: 9: 10)cm/3 (3: 3 ½: 3 ½: 4)in.
Cast off.

TO MAKE UP

Join shoulder seams. Sew in sleeves. Join sleeve seams. Sew on front bands and collar in place, then join back seam of collar. Sew on buttons. Place side belts where desired at each side and secure in position with buttons.

Right: Navy and Cream Striped Top (see page 87) and Ribbed Denim Sweater (see page 23).

Navy and Cream Striped Top

MATERIALS

3 (4: 5: 6: 7: 8) 50g balls of Rowan Cotton Glace in each of Navy (A) and Cream (B).
Pair of 2 ¾mm (No 12/US 2) knitting needles.
Pair of 3 ¼mm (No 10/US 3) double pointed knitting needles.
3 (3: 4: 4: 5: 5) buttons.

TENSION

25 sts and 36 rows to 10cm/4in square over st st on 3 ¼mm (No 10/US 3) needles.

ABBREVIATIONS

see page 8.

BACK

With 2 ¾mm (No 12/US 2) needles and A, cast on 81 (89: 105: 115: 127: 139) sts.
K 7 rows.
Change to 3 ¼ (No 10/US 3) needles.
Next row (right side) K4, turn.
Work on these 4 sts only.
K 5 (5: 9: 9: 13: 13) rows.
Leave these sts on a safety pin.
With right side facing, join B to rem sts, k to last 4 sts, turn.
Work on this set of sts only in stripe patt as follows:
1st row Return to beg of last row, with A, k to end.
2nd row With B, p to end.
3rd row Return to beg of last row, with A, p to end.
4th row With B, k to end.
The last 4 rows form stripe patt. Patt a further 1 (1: 5: 5: 9: 9) rows.
Leave these sts on a spare needle.
With right side facing, rejoin A to rem 4 sts and k 6 (6: 10: 10: 14: 14) rows.
Slip these sts onto needle holding center sts.
With wrong side facing and B, p across all sts.
Beg with a 3rd row, cont in stripe patt until Back measures approximately 22 (26: 30: 36: 39: 43)cm/8 ¾ (10 ¼: 11 ¾: 14 ¼: 15 ¼: 17)in from beg, ending with 3rd row of stripe patt. **
Next row With B, k6, p5, k to last 11 sts, p5, k6.

MEASUREMENTS

To fit age	1	1-2	3-4	4-6	6–8	8-10	years
Actual chest	64	71	84	92	102	111	cm
measurement	25	28	33	36	40	43 ½	in
Length	32	37	44	51	56	62	cm
	12 ¾	14 ½	17 ½	20 ¼	22	24 ½	in
Sleeve seam	20	23	28	32	38	40	cm
	8	9	11	12 ½	15	15 ¾	in

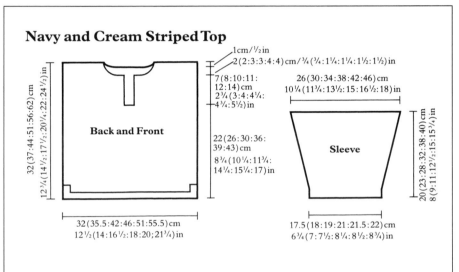

Navy and Cream Striped Top

Next row Return to beg of last row, with A, k6, p5, k to last 11 sts, p5, k6.
Next row With B, p6, k5, p to last 11 sts, k5, p6.
Next row Return to beg of last row, with A, p6, k5, p to last 11 sts, k5, p6.
Rep last 4 rows for a further 6 (7: 9: 10: 11: 13)cm/2 ¼ (2 ¾: 3 ½: 4: 4 ¼: 5)in, ending with 4th row of the last 4 rows.
Beg with 4th row, work in stripe patt until Back measures approximately 31 (36: 43: 50: 55: 61)cm/12 ¼ (14: 17: 19 ¾: 21 ½: 24)in from beg, ending with 3rd row of stripe patt.

Shape Neck
Next row Patt 29 (32: 39: 43: 48: 53), turn. Work on this set of sts only. Dec one st at neck edge on next 4 rows. 25 (28: 35: 39: 44: 49) sts.
Patt one row. Cast off.
With right side facing, slip center 23 (25: 27: 29: 31: 33) sts onto a holder, rejoin yarn to rem sts, patt to end.
Complete as given for first side.

FRONT
Work as given for Back to ★★.

Divide for opening
Next row With B, k6, p5, k27 (31: 39: 43: 49: 55), turn.
Work on this set of sts only.
Next row Return to beg of last row, with A, k6, p5, k to end.
Next row With B, p to last 11 sts, k5, p6.
Next row Return to beg of last row, with A, p to last 11 sts, k5, p6.
Next row With B, k6, p5, k to end.
Rep last 4 rows for a further 6 (7: 9: 10: 11: 13)cm/2 ¼ (2 ¾: 3 ½: 4: 4 ¼: 5)in, ending with 3rd row of the last 4 rows.
Beg with 4th row, cont in stripe patt, work 2 rows.

Shape Neck
Cast off 7 (8: 8: 8: 9: 9) sts at beg of next row.
Dec one st at neck edge on every row until 25 (28: 35: 39: 44: 49) sts rem.
Cont straight until Front matches Back to cast off edge. Cast off.
With right side facing, rejoin B to rem sts, cast off center 5 (5: 5: 7: 7: 7) sts, k to last 11 sts, p5, k6.
Next row Return to beg of last row, with A, k to last 11 sts, p5, k6.
Next row With B, p6, k5, p to end.
Next row Return to beg of last row, with A, p6, k5, p to end.
Next row With B, k to last 11 sts, p5, k6.
Complete to match first side, reversing shaping.

SLEEVES
With 2 ¾mm (No 12/US 2) needles and A, cast on 40 (42: 44: 48: 50: 52) sts.
K 7 rows, inc 4 sts evenly across last row. 44 (46: 48: 52: 54: 56) sts.
Change to 3 ¼mm (No 10/US 3) needles. Work in stripe patt as given for Back, inc one st at each end of 3rd row and every foll 5th (4th: 4th: 4th: 4th: 4th) row until there are 66 (76: 86: 96: 106: 116) sts.
Cont straight until Sleeve measures 20 (23: 28: 32: 38: 40)cm/8 (9: 11: 12 ½: 15: 15 ¾)in from beg.
Cast off.

BUTTONHOLE BAND
With 2 ¾mm (No 12/US 2) needles, A and right side facing, k up 18 (21: 26: 30: 33: 38) sts evenly along right edge of front opening.
K 2 (2: 2: 3: 3: 3) rows.
Buttonhole row K5 (6: 5: 5: 3: 4), [yf, k2 tog, k6 (7: 6: 7: 6: 7)] 1 (1: 2: 2: 3: 3) times, yf, k2 tog, k to end.
K 3 (3: 3: 4: 4: 4) rows. Cast off.

BUTTON BAND
Work to match Buttonhole Band, omitting buttonholes.

NECKBAND
Join shoulder seams.
With 2 ¾mm (No 12/US 2) needles, A and right side facing, k up 19 (20: 22: 22: 25: 25) sts up right front neck, 6 sts down right back neck, k center back neck sts dec 2 sts, k up 6 sts up left back neck and 19 (20: 22: 22: 25: 25) sts down left front neck. 71 (75: 81: 83: 91: 93) sts.
K 2 rows.
Buttonhole row
K to last 4 sts, k2 tog, yf, k2.
K 3 rows. Cast off.

TO MAKE UP
Sew side edge edgings to main part. Sew on sleeves, placing center of sleeves to shoulder seams. Beginning at top of side edgings, join side seams, then sleeve seams. Lap buttonhole band over button band and catch together row end edges to base of opening.
Sew on buttons.

Garter-stitch Jacket

MATERIALS
4 (4: 5: 5: 6) 100g hanks of Rowan Magpie Aran.
Small amount of DK yarn in Brown for embroidery.
Pair of 4 ½mm (No 7/US 7) knitting needles.
6 buttons.

TENSION
18 sts and 38 rows to 10cm/4in square over garter st (every row k) on 4 ½mm (No 7/US 7) needles.

ABBREVIATIONS
See page 8.

BACK
With 4 ½mm (No 7/US 7) needles cast on 70 (74: 78: 82: 86) sts.
Work in garter st until Back measures 33 (35: 37: 39: 41)cm/13 (13 ¾: 14 ½: 15 ¼: 16 ¼)in from beg.

Shape Neck
★★ Next 2 rows K26 (27: 28: 30: 31), sl 1, yf, turn, sl 1, k to end.
Next 2 rows K23 (24: 25: 27: 28), sl 1, yf, turn, sl 1, k to end.
Next 2 rows k20 (21: 22: 24: 25), sl 1, yf, turn, sl 1, k to end.
K 1 row across all sts.★★
Rep from ★★ to ★★. Cast off.

POCKET LININGS (make 2)
With 4 ½mm (No 7/US 7) needles cast on 23 (24: 25: 27: 28) sts.
K 22 (24: 26: 28: 30) rows.
Leave these sts on a spare needle.

MEASUREMENTS

To fit age	2-3	3-4	4-6	6–8	8-10	years
Actual chest	78	82	86	91	96	cm
measurement	31	32	34	36	38	in
Length	35	37	39	41	43	cm
	13 ¾	14 ½	15 ¼	16	17	in
Sleeve seam	22	24	27	32	40	cm
	8 ¾	9 ¾	10 ¾	12 ¾	15 ¾	in

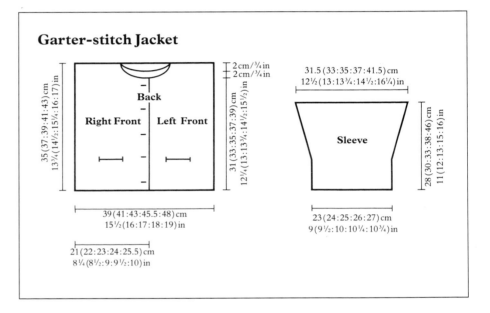

Garter-stitch Jacket

LEFT FRONT

With 4 ½mm (No 7/US 7) needles, cast on
38 (40: 42: 44: 46) sts.
K 37 (39: 41: 43: 45) rows.

Place Pocket

Next row (wrong side) K9 (9: 10: 10: 10),
cast off next 23 (24: 25: 27: 28) sts, k to end.
Next row K6 (7: 7: 7: 8), k across sts of
pocket lining, k to end.
Cont in garter st across all sts until Front
measures 31 (33: 35: 37: 39)cm/12 ¼ (13:
13 ¾: 14 ½: 15 ½)in from beg, ending with
a wrong side row.

Shape Neck

1st row K29 (30: 31: 33: 34), sl 1, yf, turn.
2nd row and 5 foll alt rows Sl 1, k to end.
3rd row K27 (28: 29: 31: 32), sl 1, yf, turn.
5th row K25 (26: 27: 29: 30), sl 1, yf, turn.
7th row K23 (24: 25: 27: 28), sl 1, yf, turn.
9th row K22 (23: 24: 26: 27), sl 1, yf, turn.
11th row K21 (22: 23: 25: 26), sl 1, yf, turn.
13th row K20 (21: 22: 24: 25) sl 1, yf, turn.
14th row As 2nd row.
K 2 rows across all sts. Cast off.
Mark front edge to indicate position of 6
buttons: first one 4 rows up from lower
edge, last one 2 rows below neck shaping
and rem 4 evenly spaced between.

RIGHT FRONT

With 4 ½mm (No 7/US 7) needles cast on
38 (40: 42: 44: 46) sts.
K 4 rows.
Buttonhole row (right side) K3, yf, k2
tog, k to end.
Complete as given for Left Front, making
buttonholes to match markers, ending with
a right side row before shaping neck and
placing pocket as follows:
Next row (wrong side) K6 (7: 7: 7: 8), cast
off next 23 (24: 25: 27: 28) sts, k to end.
Next row K9 (9: 10: 10: 10), k across sts of
pocket lining, k to end.

SLEEVES

With 4 ½mm (No 7/US 7) needles cast on
41 (43: 45: 47: 49) sts.
Work in garter st for 12cm/4 ¾in.
Cont in garter st, inc one st at each end of
next row and every foll 6th (7th: 7th: 9th: 9th)
row until there are 57 (59: 63: 67: 75) sts.
Cont straight until Sleeve measures 28 (30:
33: 38: 46)cm/11 (12: 13: 15: 18)in from beg.
Cast off.

TO MAKE UP

Join shoulder seams. Sew on sleeves,
placing center of sleeves to shoulder seams.
Join side and sleeve seams, reversing seam
on cuffs. Turn back cuffs. Catch down
pocket linings. Sew on buttons. With
Brown, embroider cross stitch on cuffs
and pockets.

Right: Garter-stitch Jacket and Simple Sweater
with Shoulder Seam Detail (see page 95).

Simple Sweater with Shoulder Seam Detail

MATERIALS
4 (4: 5: 5: 6: 6) 100g hanks of Rowan
Magpie Aran.
Pair of 4 ½mm (No 7/US 7) knitting needles.

TENSION
18 sts and 26 rows to 10cm/4in square over
st st on 4 ½mm (No 7/US 7) needles.

ABBREVIATIONS
See page 8.

MEASUREMENTS

To fit age	2-3	3-4	4-6	6–8	8-9	9-10	years
Actual chest	78	84	91	95	104	113	cm
measurement	30 ½	33	36	37 ½	41	44 ½	in
Length	43	46	49	53	57	60	cm
	17	18	19 ¼	21	22 ½	23 ½	in
Sleeve seam	28	30	32	37	40	42	cm
	11	11 ¾	12 ½	14 ½	15 ¾	16 ½	in

BACK
With 4 ½mm (No 7/US 7) needles cast on
70 (76: 82: 86: 94: 102) sts.
Work in st st until Back measures 43 (46:
49: 53: 57: 60)cm/17 (18: 19 ¼: 21: 22 ½:
23 ½)in from beg, ending with a p row.
Leave these sts on a spare needle.

FRONT
Work as given for Back until Front is 12
(12: 12: 14: 14: 14) rows less than Back,
ending with a p row.

Shape Neck
Next row K30 (33: 35: 36: 39: 42), turn.
Work on this set of sts only.
Cast off 3 sts at beg of next row.
Dec one st at neck edge on every row until
22 (24: 26: 27: 30: 33) sts rem.
Work 5 (4: 4: 6: 6: 6) rows straight.
Leave these sts on a spare needle.
With right side facing, slip center 10 (10:
12: 14: 16: 18) sts onto a holder, rejoin yarn
to rem sts and k to end.
P 1 row. Complete to match first side.

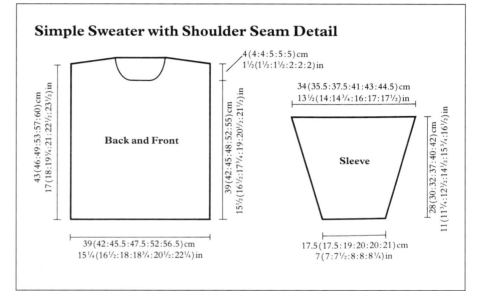

Simple Sweater with Shoulder Seam Detail

Back and Front

Sleeve

43(46:49:53:57:60)cm
17(18:19¼:21:22½:23½)in

39(42:45:48:52:55)cm
15½(16½:17¾:19:20½:21½)in

4(4:4:5:5:5)cm
1½(1½:1½:2:2:2)in

39(42:45.5:47.5:52:56.5)cm
15¼(16½:18:18¾:20½:22¼)in

34(35.5:37.5:41:43:44.5)cm
13½(14:14¾:16:17:17½)in

28(30:32:37:40:42)cm
11(11¾:12½:14½:15¾:16½)in

17.5(17.5:19:20:20:21)cm
7(7:7½:8:8:8¼)in

SLEEVES
With 4 ½mm (No 7/US 7) needles cast on
32 (32: 34: 36: 36: 38) sts.
Work in st st, inc one st at each end of 7th
row and every foll 4th row until there are 62
(64: 68: 74: 78: 82) sts.
Cont straight until Sleeve measures 28 (30:
32: 37: 40: 42)cm/11 (11 ¾: 12 ½: 14 ½:
15 ¾: 16 ½)in from beg.
Cast off.

NECKBAND
Place 22 (24: 26: 27: 30: 33) sts of right
back shoulder onto separate needle. With
wrong sides of back and front together and
right side of front facing, k tog right
shoulder sts, then cast off.
With 4 ½mm (No 7/US 7) needles and
right side facing, k up 13 (13: 13: 15: 15:
15) sts down left front neck, k center front
sts, k up 13 (13: 13: 15: 15: 15) sts up right
front neck, then k26 (28: 30: 32: 34: 36) sts
of center back neck, turn. 62 (64: 68: 76:
80: 84) sts.
Beg with a p row, work 9 (9: 9: 11: 11: 11)
rows in st st.
Cast off loosely.

TO MAKE UP
Join together left shoulder in same way as
right shoulder, then join neckband seam,
reversing seam on last 5 rows. Sew on
sleeves, placing center of sleeves to
shoulder seams. Join side and sleeve seams,
reversing seams on first and last 4 rows.

Squirrel Jacket

MATERIALS
2 (3: 4: 5) 100g hanks of Rowan Magpie Aran in Brown (A).
2 (3: 3: 3) hanks of same in Cream (B).
1 (2: 2: 2) hanks of same in Black (C).
Pair each of 4mm (No 8/US 6) and 4 ½mm (No 7/US 7) knitting needles.
35 (40: 45: 50) cm/14 (16:18:20) in long open ended zip fastener.

TENSION
18 sts and 23 rows to 10cm/4in square over pattern on 4 ½mm (No 7/US 7) needles.

ABBREVIATIONS
See page 8.

NOTES
Read charts from right to left on right side rows and from left to right on wrong side rows unless otherwise stated. When working in color pattern, strand yarn not in use loosely across wrong side to keep fabric elastic. When working squirrel motifs, use separate small balls for each colored area and twist yarns together on wrong side at joins to avoid holes.

BACK
With 4mm (No 8/US 6) needles and A, cast on 74 (82: 90: 102) sts.
1st rib row (right side) K2, [p2, k2] to end.
2nd rib row P2, [k2, p2] to end.
Rib 2 rows in C and 2 rows in A.
Change to 4 ½mm (No 7/US 7) needles.
Beg with a k row, cont in st st throughout, work 6 (8: 10: 12) rows in A.
Work 11 rows of chart 1.
With A, work 9 (13: 17: 21) rows.
Change to B and work 1 row.
Work 3 rows of chart 2.
With B, work 3 rows.
Next row P3 (6: 9: 14)B, reading chart from right to left (thus reversing motif), p 1st row of chart 3, p12 (14: 16: 18)B, reading chart from left to right, p 1st row of chart 3, p3 (6: 9: 14)B.
Next row K3 (6: 9: 14)B, reading chart from right to left, k 2nd row of chart 3, k12 (14: 16: 18)B, reading chart from left to right, k 2nd row of chart 3, k3 (6: 9: 14)B.
Work a further 22 rows as set.
With B, work 3 rows.
Work 3rd row, then 2nd and 1st rows of chart 2.
With B, work 1 row.

MEASUREMENTS

To fit age	4	6	8	10	years
Actual chest measurement	82	91	100	113	cm
	32	36	39 ½	44 ½	in
Length	44	49	54	59	cm
	17 ¼	19 ¼	21 ¼	23 ¼	in
Sleeve seam	30	33	36	40	cm
	11 ¾	13	14	15 ¾	in

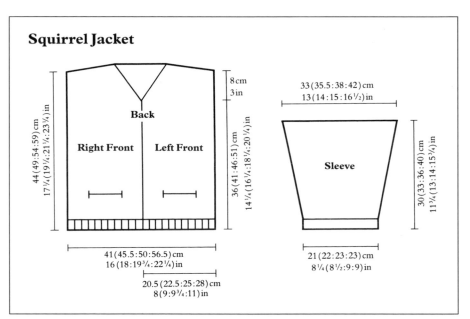

Squirrel Jacket

With A, work 10 (14: 18: 24) rows.
Work 9 rows of chart 4.
Cont in A only until Back measures 44 (49: 54: 59)cm/17 ¼ (19 ¼: 21 ¼: 23 ¼)in from beg, ending with a wrong side row.

Shape Shoulders
Cast off 13 (14: 16: 18) sts at beg of next 2 rows and 13 (15: 16: 19) sts at beg of foll 2 rows.
Cast off rem 22 (24: 26: 28) sts.

POCKET LININGS (make 2)
With 4 ½mm (No 7/US 7) needles and A, cast on 20 (20: 22: 22) sts.
Beg with a k row, work 24 (26: 28: 30) rows in st st.
Leave these sts on a holder.

LEFT FRONT

With 4mm (No 8/US 6) needles and A, cast on 37 (41: 45: 49) sts.

1st rib row (right side) K2, [p2, k2] to last 3 sts, k3.

2nd rib row K3, p2, [k2, p2] to end.

** Using small separate ball of A for the 3 sts at front edge and twisting yarns together on wrong side at joins, work as follows:

Rib 2 rows in C and 2 rows in A, inc 2 sts evenly across last row on 4th size only. 37 (41: 45: 51) sts.

Change to 4 ½mm (No 7/US 7) needles.

Keeping the 3 sts at front edge in garter st (every row k) and A and remainder in st st throughout, cont as follows:

With A and beg with a k row, work 6 (8: 10: 12) rows.

Work 11 rows of chart 1.

Cont in A only, work 2 rows. **

Next row K3, p7 (9: 10: 13), k20 (20: 22: 22), p7 (9: 10: 13).

Next row K.

Rep last 2 rows once more.

Next row K3, p7 (9: 10: 13), cast off knitwise next 20 (20: 22: 22) sts, p to end.

Place Pocket

Next row K7 (9: 10: 13), k across sts of pocket lining, k to end.

Work 1 (5: 9: 13) rows.

Change to B and work 1 row.

Work 3 rows of chart 2.

With B, work 3 rows.

Next row K3A, p3 (4: 6: 9)B, reading chart from left to right p 1st row of chart 3, p3 (6: 8: 11)B.

Next row K3 (6: 8: 11)B, reading chart from right to left, k 2nd row of chart 3, k3 (4: 6: 9)B, 3A.

Work a further 22 rows as set.

With B, work 3 rows. Work 3rd row, then 2nd and 1st rows of chart 2.

With B, work 1 row.

With A, work 10 (14: 18: 24) rows.

Work 4 rows of chart 4.

Shape Neck

Next row Patt to last 3 sts, turn; leave the 3 sts on a safety pin.

Keeping patt correct, dec one st at neck edge on next 4 rows.

Cont in A only, dec one st at neck edge on every row until 26 (29: 32: 37) sts rem.

Cont straight until front matches Back to shoulder shaping, ending with a wrong side row.

Shape Shoulder

Cast off 13 (14: 16: 18) sts at beg of next row.

Work 1 row. Cast off rem 13 (15: 16: 19) sts.

RIGHT FRONT

With 4mm (No 8/US 6) needles and A, cast on 37 (41: 45: 49) sts.

1st rib row (right side) K5, [p2, k2] to end.

2nd rib row P2, [k2, p2] to last 3 sts, k3.

Work as given for Left Front from ** to **.

Next row P7 (9: 10: 13), k20 (20: 22: 22), p7 (9: 10: 13), k3.

Next row K.

Rep last 2 rows once more.

Next row P7 (9: 10: 13), cast off knitwise next 20 (20: 22: 22) sts, p to last 3 sts, k3.

Place Pocket

Next row K10 (12: 13: 16), k across sts of pocket lining, k to end.

Work 1 (5: 9: 13) rows.

Change to B and work 1 row.

Work 3 rows of chart 2.

With B, work 3 rows.

Next row P3 (6: 8: 11)B, reading chart from right to left, p 1st row of chart 3, p3 (4: 6: 9)B, k3A.

Next row K3A, 3 (4: 6: 9)B, reading chart from left to right, k 2nd row of chart 3, k3 (6: 9: 11)B.

Complete to match Left Front, reversing shapings.

LEFT SLEEVE

With 4mm (No 8/US 6) needles and A, cast on 38 (38: 42: 42) sts.

Work 2 rows in rib as given for Back.

Rib 2 rows in C and 2 rows in A, inc 2 sts evenly across last row on 2nd size only. 38 (40: 42: 42) sts.

Change to 4 ½mm (No 7/US 7) needles.

Beg with a k row, cont in st st, work 2 rows.

Work 11 rows of chart 1 as indicated for Back, **at the same time,** inc one st at each end of 1st and 3 foll 3rd rows, working inc sts into pattern. 46 (48: 50: 50) sts.

With A, work 9 (13: 17: 21) rows, inc one st at each end of every 3rd row. 52 (56: 60: 64) sts.

With B, work 1 row.

Work 3 rows of chart 2 as indicated for 4th size of Left Front.

With B, work 3 rows, inc one st at each end of 1st row. 54 (58: 62: 66) sts.

Next row P13 (15: 17: 19), reading chart from left to right, p 1st row of chart 3, with B, p to end.

Next row Inc in first st, k12 (14: 16: 18)B, reading chart from right to left, k 2nd row of chart 3, with B, k to last st, inc in last st. Work a further 22 rows as set, inc one st at each end of 2 (2: 2: 4) foll 4th rows. 60 (64: 68: 76) sts.

With B, work 3 rows.

Work 3rd row, then 2nd and 1st rows of chart 2.

With B, work 1 row.

Cont in A only until Sleeve measures 30 (33: 36: 40)cm/11 ¾ (13: 14: 15 ¾)in from beg, ending with a wrong side row.

Cast off.

RIGHT SLEEVE

Work as given for Left Sleeve, reversing squirrel motif by reading chart from left to right on right side rows and from right to left on wrong side rows.

LEFT COLLAR

With 4mm (No 8/US 6) needles, rejoin A at inside edge to 3 sts on left front safety pin.

Work 12 rows in garter st, inc one st at inside edge on every 2nd row.

Cont inc one st at inside edge as before, work 6 rows C, 6 rows A, 6 rows C, then cont in A only until there are 27 sts, ending at outside edge.

Shape Collar

Next 2 rows K14, yf, sl 1, yb, turn, sl 1, yb, k to end.

K 4 rows.

Rep last 6 rows until Collar fits up front neck to center of back neck, ending at outside edge.

Cast off.

RIGHT COLLAR

Work to match Left Collar.

TO MAKE UP

Join shoulder seams. Sew on sleeves, placing center of sleeves to shoulder seams. Join side and sleeve seams. Sew on collar, then join back seam. Catch down pocket linings. Sew in zip fastener.

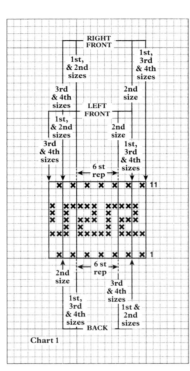

Chart 1

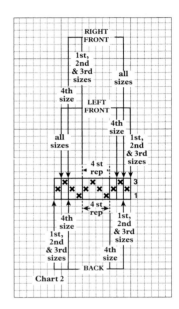

Chart 2

KEY

☐ Cream (B)

☒ Black (C)

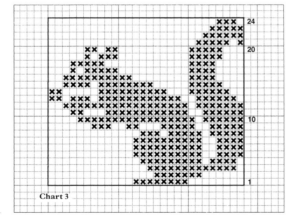

Chart 3

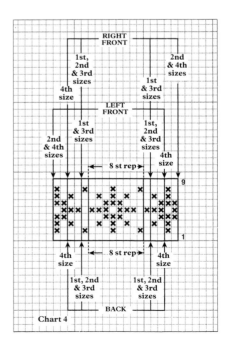

Chart 4

Tweed Jacket with Cable Beret

MATERIALS

Jacket 6 (7: 8) 50g hanks of Rowan DK Tweed.
Pair of 4mm (No 8/US 6) knitting needles.
Cable needle.
8 buttons.
Beret 2 50g hanks of Rowan DK Tweed.
Pair of 4mm (No 8/US 6) knitting needles.
Cable needle.

TENSION

25 sts and 34 rows to 10cm/4in square over pattern on 4mm (No 8/US 6) needles.

ABBREVIATIONS

C6F = sl next 3 sts onto cable needle and leave at front of work, k3, then k3 from cable needle;
C4F = sl next 2 sts onto cable needle and leave at front of work, k2, then k2 from cable needle;
Also see page 8.

JACKET
BACK

With 4mm (No 8/US 6) needles cast on 89 (97: 111) sts.
1st row (right side) P1, [k1, p1] 1 (3: 1) times, k6, *p1, [k1, p1] twice, k6; rep from * to last 3 (7: 3) sts, p1, [k1, p1] 1 (3: 1) times.
2nd row [P1, k1] 1 (3: 1) times, p8, *k1, p1, k1, p8; rep from * to last 2 (6: 2) sts, [k1, p1] 1 (3: 1) times.
3rd and 4th rows As 1st and 2nd rows.
5th row P1, [k1, p1] 1 (3: 1) times, C6F, *p1, [k1, p1] twice, C6F; rep from * to last 3 (7: 3) sts, p1, [k1, p1] 1 (3, 1) times.
6th row As 2nd row.
7th and 8th rows As 1st and 2nd rows.
These 8 rows form patt.
Cont in patt until Back measures 19 (21: 24)cm/7 ½ (8 ¼: 9 ½)in from beg, ending with a wrong side row.

Shape Armholes

Cast off 8 (5: 8) sts at beg of next 2 rows. 73 (87: 95) sts.
Cont straight until Back measures 36 (40: 45)cm/14 ¼ (15 ¾: 17 ¾)in from beg, ending with a wrong side row.

Shape Shoulders

Cast off 10 (12: 14) sts at beg of next 2 rows and 10 (13: 14) sts at beg of foll 2 rows.
Cast off rem 33 (37: 39) sts.

MEASUREMENTS

JACKET

To fit age	2-3	3-5	5-7	years
Actual chest measurement	72	80	90	cm
	28 ½	31 ½	35 ½	in
Length	39	43	48	cm
	15 ½	17	19	in
Sleeve seam	25	28	33	cm
	10	11	13	in

BERET

To fit average child's head.

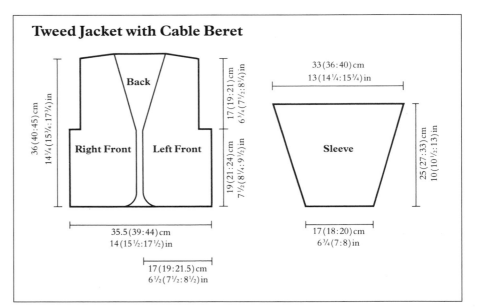

Tweed Jacket with Cable Beret

Back
Right Front   Left Front

36 (40: 45) cm
14 ¼ (15 ¾: 17 ¾) in

17 (19: 21) cm
6 ¾ (7 ½: 8 ¼) in

19 (21: 24) cm
7 ½ (8 ¼: 9 ½) in

35.5 (39: 44) cm
14 (15 ½: 17 ½) in

17 (19: 21.5) cm
6 ½ (7 ½: 8 ½) in

Sleeve

33 (36: 40) cm
13 (14 ¼: 15 ¾) in

25 (27: 33) cm
10 (10 ½: 13) in

17 (18: 20) cm
6 ¾ (7: 8) in

LEFT FRONT

With 4mm (No 8/US 6) needles cast on 30 (34: 41) sts.

1st row (right side) P1, [k1, p1] 1 (3: 1) times, *k6, p1, [k1, p1] twice; rep from * to last 5 sts, k5.

2nd row Cast on 2, p8, *k1, p1, k1, p8; rep from * to last 2 (6: 2) sts, [k1, p1] 1 (3: 1) times.

3rd row P1, [k1, p1] 1 (3: 1) times, k6, *p1, [k1, p1] twice, k6; rep from * to last st, p1, k1 in last st.

4th row Cast on 2, k1, p1, k1, p8, *k1, p1, k1, p8; rep from * to last 2 (6: 2) sts, [k1, p1] 1 (3: 1) times.

5th row P1, [k1, p1] 1 (3: 1) times, C6F, *p1, [k1, p1] twice, C6F; rep from * to last 4 sts, p1, k1, p1, then k1, p1 in last st.

6th row Cast on 2, p3, k1, p1, k1, p8, *k1, p1, k1, p8; rep from * to last 2 (6: 2) sts, [k1, p1] 1 (3: 1) times.

7th row P1, [k1, p1] 1 (3: 1) times, *k6, p1, [k1, p1] twice; rep from * to last 2 sts, k1, k twice in last st.

8th row P twice in first st, p3, *k1, p1, k1, p8; rep from * to last 2 (6: 2) sts, [k1, p1] 1 (3: 1) times.

These 8 rows set patt.

Cont in patt as set, inc one st at end of next row and at same edge on foll 2 rows. 43 (47: 54) sts.

Work straight until Front matches Back to armhole shaping, ending with a wrong side row.

Shape Armhole and Neck

Cast off 8 (5: 8) sts at beg of next row. Keeping armhole edge straight and patt correct, dec one st at neck edge on 2nd row and every foll 3rd row until 20 (25: 28) sts rem.

Cont straight until Front matches Back to shoulder shaping, ending with a wrong side row.

Shape Shoulder

Cast off 10 (12: 14) sts at beg of next row. Patt 1 row. Cast off rem 10 (13: 14) sts.

RIGHT FRONT

With 4mm (No 8/US 6) needles cast on 30 (34: 41) sts.

1st row (right side) K5, *p1, [k1, p1] twice, k6; rep from * to last 3 (7: 3) sts, p1, [k1, p1] 1 (3: 1) times.

2nd row [P1, k1] 1 (3: 1) times, *p8, k1, p1, k1; rep from * to last 6 sts, p5, p twice in last st.

3rd row Cast on 2, k1, p1, k6, *p1, [k1, p1] twice, k6; rep from * to last 3 (7: 3) sts, p1, [k1, p1] 1 (3: 1) times.

4th row [P1, k1] 1 (3: 1) times, p8, *k1, p1, k1, p8; rep from * to last st, k1, p1 in last st.

5th row Cast on 2, *p1, [k1, p1] twice, C6F; rep from * to last 3 (7: 3) sts, p1, [k1, p1] 1 (3: 1) times.

6th row [P1, k1] 1 (3: 1) times, *p8, k1, p1, k1; rep from * to last st, p twice in last st.

7th row Cast on 2, k3, *p1, [k1, p1] twice, k6; rep from * to last 3 (7: 3) sts, p1, [k1, p1] 1 (3: 1) times.

8th row [P1, k1] 1 (3: 1) times, *p8, k1, p1, k1; rep from * to last 4 sts, p3, p twice in last st.

These 8 rows set patt.

Complete to match Left Front, reversing shapings.

SLEEVES

With 4mm (No 8, US 6) needles, cast on 42 (46: 50) sts.

1st row (right side) K2 (4: 6), p1, [k1, p1] twice, *k6, p1, [k1, p1] twice; rep from * to last 2 (4: 6) sts, k to end.

2nd row P3 (5: 7), k1, p1, k1, *p8, k1, p1, k1; rep from * to last 3 (5: 7) sts, p to end.

These 2 rows set patt.

Cont in patt, inc one st at each end of 3rd row and 5 foll alt rows, then on every foll 4th row until there are 82 (90: 100) sts, working inc sts into patt.

Cont straight until Sleeve measures 25 (27: 33)cm/10 (10 ½: 13)in from beg, ending with a wrong side row.

Cast off.

BACK WELT

With 4mm (No 8/US 6) needles cast on 7 sts.

1st row K1, [p1, k1] to end.

This row forms moss st patt. Cont in moss st until band, when slightly stretched, fits along lower edge of back.

Cast off.

LEFT FRONT WELT, BUTTON BAND AND COLLAR

Join shoulder seams.

With 4mm (No 8/US 6) needles cast on 7 sts.

Work in moss st as given for Back Welt, until band fits along cast on edge of Left Front, easing band round lower shaped edge and up straight edge to beg of neck shaping.

Shape Collar

Cont in moss st, inc one st at beg of next row and at same edge on every foll 3rd row until there are 21 sts.

Work straight until shaped edge of Collar fits up front neck to shoulder, ending at straight edge.

Next 2 rows Moss st 14, sl 1, yf, turn, sl 1, moss st to end.

Moss st 4 rows.

Rep last 6 rows until shaped edge of Collar fits up front neck to center of back neck.

Cast off.

Sew welt, band and collar in place.

Mark band along straight edge to indicate position of 4 buttons: first one 1cm/ ¼in above lower edge shaping, last one 1cm/ ¼in below beg of collar shaping and rem 2 evenly spaced between.

RIGHT FRONT WELT, BUTTONHOLE BAND AND COLLAR

Work as given for Left Front Welt, Button Band and Collar, making buttonholes at markers as follows:

Buttonhole row Moss st 2, cast off 3, moss st to end.

Next row Moss st 2, cast on 3, moss st 2.

SLEEVE CUFFS (make 2)

Work as given for Back Welt until band fits along lower edge of Sleeve.

Cast off.

SIDE BELTS (make 2)

With 4mm (No 8/US 6) needles cast on 7 sts.

Work in moss st as given for Back Welt for 9cm/3 ½in.

Dec one st at each end of next 2 rows.

Work 3 tog and fasten off.

TO MAKE UP

Join back seam of collar. Sew on back welt and sleeve cuffs. Sew on sleeves, placing center of sleeves to shoulder seams and sewing last 3 (2: 3)cm/1 ¼ (¾: 1 ¼)in of sleeve tops to cast off sts at armholes. Join side and sleeve seams. Place side belts at sides and secure each end of belt in position with button.

Sew on buttons.

BERET

With 4mm (No 8/US 6) needles cast on 73 sts.

1st row K1, [p1, k1] to end.

This row forms moss st.

Moss st 6 rows.

Inc row Inc in first st, moss st 3, *[m1, moss st 1] 3 times, moss st 2, work 3 times in next st, moss st 3; rep from * to last 6 sts, [m1, moss st 1] 3 times, moss st 2, work twice in last st. 113 sts.

1st row (right side) [Moss st 4, k6, moss st 4] to last st, moss st 1.

2nd row Moss st 1, [moss st 4, p6, moss st 4] to end.

3rd (inc) row [Moss st 4, m1, k6, m1, moss st 4] to last st, moss st 1.

4th row Moss st 1, [moss st 5, p6, moss st 5] to end.

5th (inc) row [Moss st 5, m1, C6F, m1, moss st 5] to last st, moss st 1.

6th row Moss st 1, [moss st 6, p6, moss st 6] to end.

7th (inc) row [Moss st 6, m1, k6, m1, moss st 6] to last st, moss st 1.

8th row Moss st 1, [moss st 7, p6, moss st 7] to end.

These 8 rows set patt.

Inc row [Patt 7, m1, patt 6, m1, patt 7] to last st, patt 1.

Patt 3 rows straight.

Inc row [Patt 8, m1, patt 6, m1, patt 8] to last st, patt 1.

Patt 3 rows straight.

Inc row [Patt 9, m1, patt 6, m1, patt 9] to last st, patt 1. 209 sts.

Patt 9 rows straight.

Dec row [Patt 8, work 2 tog, patt 6, work 2 tog tbl, patt 8] to last st, patt 1.

Patt 3 rows straight.

Dec row [Patt 7, work 2 tog, patt 6, work 2 tog tbl, patt 7] to last st, patt 1.

Patt 3 rows straight.

Dec row [Patt 6, work 2 tog, patt 6, work 2 tog tbl, patt 6] to last st, patt 1.

Cont in this way, dec 16 sts as set on every foll 4th row until 97 sts rem.

Patt 3 rows straight.

Dec row [Patt 3, k2 tog, k2, k2 tog tbl, patt 3] to last st, patt 1.

Next row Patt 1, [patt 3, p4, patt 3] to end.

Next row [Patt 3, C4F, patt 3] to last st, patt 1.

Next row Patt 1, [patt 3, p4, patt 3] to end.

Dec row [Patt 1, work 2 tog, k4, work 2 tog tbl, patt 1] to last st, patt 1.

Next row Patt 1, [patt 2, p4, patt 2] to end.

Next row [Patt 2, C4F, patt 2] to last st, patt 1.

Next row Patt 1, [patt 2, p4, patt 2] to end.

Dec row [Work 2 tog, k4, work 2 tog tbl] to last st, patt 1.

Next row Patt 1, [patt 1, p4, patt 1] to end.

Dec row Patt 1, [C4F, p2 tog] to end.

P 1 row.

Dec row P1, [k2 tog, k2 tog tbl, p1] to end.

Dec row P1, [p2 tog] to end.

Break off yarn, thread end through rem 13 sts, pull up and secure. Join seam.

Black and White Fair Isle Cardigan

MATERIALS

6 (7: 8) 50g balls of Rowan DK Handknit Cotton in Black (A).
5 (5: 6) balls of same in Cream.
1 ball of same in Flame (B).
Pair each of 3 ¼mm (No 10/US 3) and 4mm (No 8/US 6) knitting needles.
One each of 3 ¼mm (No 10/US 3) and 4mm (No 8/US 6) circular knitting needles.
5 buttons.

TENSION

22 sts and 25 rows to 10cm/4in square over pattern on 4mm (No 8/US 6) needles.

ABBREVIATIONS

See page 8.

NOTES

Read chart from right to left on right side (k) rows and from left to right on wrong side (p) rows. When working in pattern, strand yarn not in use loosely across wrong side to keep fabric elastic.

BACK AND FRONTS

Worked in one piece to armholes.
With 3 ¼mm (No 10/US 3) circular needle and B, cast on 200 (224: 248) sts.
Work forwards and backwards in rows.
K 1 row.
Next row Cast off purlwise 4 sts, p to last 4 sts, cast off purlwise last 4 sts. 192 (216: 240) sts.
Change to A.
1st rib row (right side) K3, [p2, k2] to last 5 sts, p2, k3.
2nd rib row P3, [k2, p2] to last 5 sts, k2, p3.
Rep last 2 rows 3 times more, inc one st at center of last row. 193 (217: 241) sts.
Change to 4mm (No 8/US 6) circular needle.
Beg with a k row, work in st st and patt from chart until work measures 25 (28: 31)cm/ 9 ¾ (11: 12 ¼)in from beg, ending with a wrong side row.

Right Front
Next row Patt 48 (54: 60) turn.
Work on this set of sts only until work measures 28 (31: 34)cm/11 (12 ¼: 13 ½)in from beg, ending with a wrong side row.

MEASUREMENTS

To fit age	4-6	6–8	8-10	years
Actual chest measurement	89	100	111	cm
	35	39 ½	43 ½	in
Length	41	46	51	cm
	16	18	20	in
Sleeve seam	31	34	38	cm
	12 ¼	13 ½	15	in

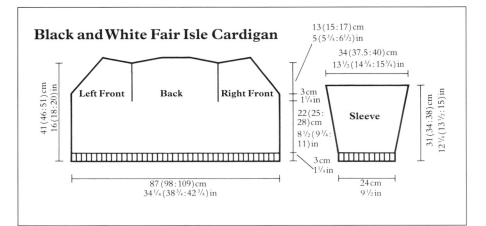

Black and White Fair Isle Cardigan

Left Front　　Back　　Right Front

41 (46: 51) cm
16 (18: 20) in

87 (98: 109) cm
34 ¼ (38 ¾: 42 ¾) in

13 (15: 17) cm
5 (5 ¾: 6 ½) in

34 (37.5: 40) cm
13 ½ (14 ¾: 15 ¾) in

3 cm
1 ¼ in

22 (25: 28) cm
8 ½ (9 ¾: 11) in

3 cm
1 ¼ in

Sleeve

31 (34: 38) cm
12 ¼ (13 ½: 15) in

24 cm
9 ½ in

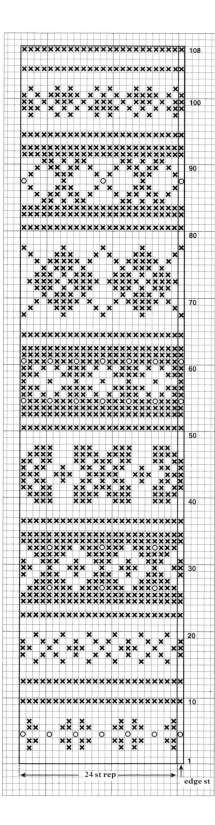

24 st rep   edge st

KEY

☐   Black (A)

☒   Cream

◧   Flame (B)

Shape Neck

Keeping patt correct, dec one st at neck edge on next 5 rows then on every foll alt row until 32 (35: 38) sts rem.
Cont straight until work measures 41 (46: 51)cm/16 (18: 20)in from beg, ending with a right side row.

Shape Shoulder

Cast off 16 (17: 19) sts at beg of next row.
Work 1 row. Cast off rem 16 (18: 19) sts.

Back

With right side facing, rejoin yarn to rem sts and patt 97 (109: 121) sts, turn.
Work on this set of sts only until work measures 41 (46: 51)cm/16 (18: 20)in from beg, ending with a wrong side row.

Shape Shoulders

Cast off 16 (17: 19) sts at beg of next 2 rows and 16 (18: 19) sts at beg of foll 2 rows.
Leave rem 33 (39: 45) sts on a holder.

Left Front

With right side facing, rejoin yarn to rem sts and patt to end.
Complete to match Right Front, but ending with a wrong side row before shaping shoulder.

SLEEVES

With 3 ¼mm (No 10/US 3) needles and B, cast on 50 sts.
K 1 row and p 1 row.
Change to A.
1st rib row (right side) K2, [p2, k2] to end.
2nd rib row P2, [k2, p2] to end.
Rep last 2 rows 3 times more, inc 3 sts evenly across last row. 53 sts.
Change to 4mm (No 8/US 6) needles.
Next row K last 3 sts of the 24 st patt rep, k the 24 sts twice, then k first 2 sts.
Next row P last 2 sts of the 24 st patt rep, p the 24 sts twice, then p the first 3 sts.
Cont working from chart as set, at the same time, inc one st at each end of 3rd row, then on every foll 5th (4th: 4th) row until there are 75 (83: 89) sts, working inc sts into patt.
Cont straight until Sleeve measures 31 (34: 38)cm/12 ¼ (13 ½: 15)in from beg, ending with a wrong side row.
Cast off.

FRONT BAND

Join shoulder seams.
With 3 ¼mm (No 10/US 3) circular needle, A and right side facing, k up 56 (60: 64) sts along straight right front edge omitting the 2 rows of B at lower edge, 39 (42: 45) sts along shaped edge to shoulder, k back neck sts, dec one st at center, k up 39 (42: 45) sts down shaped edge of left front to beg of neck shaping and 56 (60: 64) sts along straight edge omitting the 2 rows of B at lower edge. 222 (242: 262) sts.
Work backwards and forwards in rows.
Beg with a 2nd row, work 2 rows in rib as given for Sleeves.
Buttonhole row Rib to last 50 (54: 58) sts, [cast off 2, rib 8 (9: 10) sts more] 4 times, cast off 2, rib to end.
Next row Rib to end, casting on 2 sts over those cast off in previous row.
Rib 1 row. Sew the cast off sts at each end of lower edge to row ends of band.
Change to B.
Next row Pick up 2 sts from lower edge, k to end, then pick up 2 sts from lower edge.
P 1 row. Cast off with B.

TO MAKE UP

Sew in sleeves, placing center of sleeves to shoulder seams. Join sleeve seams. Sew on buttons.

Right: Black and White Fair Isle Cardigan and Simple Striped Sweater (see page 111).

Simple Striped Sweater

MATERIALS
4 (4: 5: 7: 8) 50g balls of Rowan DK
Handknit Cotton in Black (A).
3 (3: 4: 6: 7) balls of same in Cream (B).
1 (2: 2: 2: 3) balls of same in Flame (C).
Pair each of 3 ¼mm (No 10/US 3) and
4mm (No 8/US 6) knitting needles.

TENSION
20 sts and 28 rows to 10cm/4in square over
st st on 4mm (No 8/US 6) needles.

ABBREVIATIONS
See page 8.

BACK
With 4mm (No 8/US 6) needles and C, cast
on 78 (84: 90: 98: 106) sts.
Beg with a k row, work in st st and stripe
patt of 2 rows C, 2 rows B, 4 rows A, 2 rows
B, 2 rows A, 2 rows B, 4 rows A and 2 rows
B throughout until Back measures 39 (42:
46: 51: 56)cm/15 ¼ (16 ½: 18: 20: 22)in
from beg, ending with a wrong side row.

Shape Shoulders
Cast off 12 (13: 14: 15: 17) sts at beg of next
2 rows and 12 (13: 14: 16: 17) sts at beg of
foll 2 rows.
Leave rem 30 (32: 34: 36: 38) sts on a holder.

MEASUREMENTS

To fit age	2-3	3-4	4-6	6–8	8-10	years
Actual chest	78	84	90	98	106	cm
measurement	31	33	35 ½	38 ½	41 ½	in
Length	39	42	46	51	56	cm
	15 ¼	16 ½	18	20	22	in
Sleeve seam	25	28	34	38	40	cm
	10	11	13 ½	15	15 ½	in

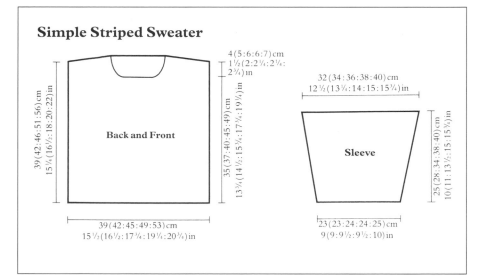

FRONT
Work as given for Back until Front
measures 35 (37: 40: 45: 49)cm/13 ¾ (14 ½:
15 ¾: 17 ¾: 19 ¼)in from beg, ending with
a wrong side row.

Shape Neck
Next row K31 (33: 35: 38: 41), turn.
Work on this set of sts only.
Dec one st at neck edge on every row until
24 (26: 28: 31: 34) sts rem.
Cont straight until Front matches Back to
shoulder shaping, ending at side edge.

Shape Shoulder
Cast off 12 (13: 14: 15: 17) sts at beg of next
row.
Work 1 row. Cast off rem 12 (13: 14: 16: 17)
sts.
With right side facing, slip center 16 (18:
20: 22: 24) sts onto a holder, rejoin yarn to
rem sts and k to end.
Complete to match first side.

SLEEVES
With 4mm (No 8/US 6) needles and C,
cast on 46 (46: 48: 48: 50) sts.
Beg with a k row, work in st st and stripe
patt as given for Back, **at the same time**,
inc one st at each end of 5th row and every
foll 6th (6th: 7th: 7th: 6th) row until there
are 64 (68: 72: 76: 80) sts.
Cont straight until Sleeve measures 25 (28:
34: 38: 40)cm/10 (11: 13 ½: 15: 15 ¾)in
from beg, ending with a wrong side row.
Cast off.

NECKBAND
Join right shoulder seam.
With 3 ¼mm (No 10/US 3) needles, A and
right side facing, pick up and k12 (14: 16:
16: 18) sts down left front neck, k center
front sts, pick up and k12 (14: 16: 16: 18)

sts up right front neck, k back neck sts. 70
(78: 86: 90: 98) sts.
Beg with a p row, work in st st and stripe
patt of 3 rows A, 2 rows B, and 2 rows C.
With C, cast off loosely.

TO MAKE UP
Join left shoulder and neckband seam,
reversing seam on last 4 rows of neckband.
Sew on sleeves, placing center of sleeves to
shoulder seams. Join side and sleeve seams,
reversing seams on first and last 4 rows.

AUTHOR'S ACKNOWLEDGEMENTS

I would like to thank the following knitters for their invaluable help: Pat Church, Tina Egleton, Penny Hill, Maisie Lawrence, Frances Wallace.

I am particularly grateful to Tina Egleton for her great skill and dedication in checking the patterns, and to Sandra Lousada, not only for the beautiful photographs but for her commitment to the project. I would like to thank Marie Willey for her lovely styling and Alison Walsh for her help on the shoot.

Thank you also to Heather Jeeves, my wonderful agent, and to Cindy Richards at Collins & Brown for creating the opportunity to work on this project.

Last, but not least, a special thank you to all the children and their parents: Ashley, Amy, Anna, Ava, Billy, Callum, Connie, Eleanor, Hannah, Caitie, Kiyomi, Lily, Leina, Sharleyne, Ollie, Omar, Mickey, Joe, Mica and Yasmin.

Clothes provided by Nipper.

SUPPLIERS/DISTRIBUTORS

Suppliers of Rowan Yarns and Jaeger Handknits

USA
Westminster Fibers, Inc.
4 Townsend West, Suite 8
Nashua, NH 03063
Tel: 603 886 5041
Fax: 603 886 1056
www.knitrowan.com
E-mail: knitting@westminsterfibers.com

Canada
Diamond Yarn
9697 St Laurent
Montreal
Quebec H3L 2N1
Tel: 514 388 6188

Diamond Yarn (Toronto)
155 Martin Ross
Unit 3
Toronto
Ontario M3J 2L9
Tel: 416 736 6111

Australia
Rowan at Sunspun
185 Canterbury Road
Canterbury
Victoria 3126
Tel: 03 9830 1609

UK
Rowan Yarns and Jaeger Handknits
Green Lane Mill
Holmfirth
West Yorkshire
HD9 2DX
Tel: 01484 681881
www.knitrowan.com

Great Knits for Kids